IN THE
SHADOW OF THE
RISING SUN

To Nora Morris, my mum, without whom
we wouldn't have survived.

IN THE SHADOW OF THE RISING SUN

SURVIVING A PRISONER OF WAR CHILDHOOD

OLGA HENDERSON

MIRROR BOOKS

m
B

MIRROR BOOKS

1

Published in Great Britain and Ireland in 2023 by
Mirror Books, a Reach PLC business.

Written with Chris Manby

www.mirrorbooks.co.uk
@TheMirrorBooks

Print ISBN 9781915306425
eBook ISBN 9781915306432

Cover Design: Rick Cooke
Editing: Christine Costello

Printed and bound in Great Britain by
CPI Group (UK) Ltd, Croydon, CR0 4YY

CONTENTS

Foreword   9
Prologue   13

Mum & Dad   16
Tigers in the Night   20
Fruit Trees and Flying Foxes   25
Parties and Pranks   29
Everybody's Children   35
Convent Girls   39
Expat Rules   43
Rumblings of War   51
War Comes to Singapore   54
Counting Planes   57

Back to School, but Not For Long   61
'You've Got Half an Hour'   65
Uncle Tom   69
Our Friends in the Army   73
'You're Not Official'   76
The Fall of Singapore   80
The 'Sook Ching'   83
Enemy Aliens   86
Katong   91
The Best and The Worst   93

The Road to Changi Jail   98

Our New Home   105
Anything You Like as Long as it's Rice   109
A Different Kind of Education   112
The Rose Garden   115
The Birthday Girl   118
A Day at the Beach   121
Ghost Stories   126
The Changi Quilts   129
Mrs Mulvany   136
Balsam and Blue Stocking   144
The Rings   147
Propaganda   153
The 'Double Tenth'   157

On the Move Again   164
The Little Match Girl   169
The 'Riff Raff'   172
Maggots and Snails   177
'She'll Pull Through'   181
The Comfort Women   185
Caught in the Act   189
Dad and Peter   194
The Pushback   199

Bread and Butter   203
The Cavalry Arrives   208
The SS Almanzora   211
'You Had it Easy'   215
Letters from 'Hoggie'   219

CONTENTS

Homesick	223
Making Do	227
Love at First Sight	231
The Convent Girl and The Courtesan	237
Wedding Bells	241
Soulmates	245
And Then There Were Four	248
The Long Shadow of War	253
More Travels with My Family	268
A Happy Ever After Cut Short	262
What Came Next	266
Keeping the Memories Alive	269
The Power of Forgiveness	273
Epilogue	278
Acknowledgements	280
Pieces of the Past	281

Foreword

BY EMMA MURRAY, OLGA'S GRANDDAUGHTER

Growing up, we were always aware that our grandmother was different to other 'nannies'. As a child, I have memories of her turning up on the driveway in her little mini, with her boot packed with as many clothes as she needed for whatever adventure awaited. Her cat Sugar (her patient and tolerant travelling companion) would be in the back seat of the car, completely accepting of whichever household she was about to become a temporary resident of. These visits could last days, weeks or months. My grandmother would help to decorate, rearrange cupboards (sometimes without my mum's permission) and tell us stories.

It was during these visits that the difference between mine and my school friends' families was clear. Other children were read fairy tales and Enid Blyton. We were exposed to stories that not even my sneaking teenage glimpses of Stephen King could rival: we were told of a place called 'Camp'. These stories could vary wildly in their themes and levels of terror invoked. Some stories were of comradery and collaboration and others would make, I'm sure, even the most hardened adult wince.

I remember being fascinated by the 'bugs in the blanket' story. This memory shared by my Grandmother involved telling us all about the hundreds of lice and insects (and their sizes – shudder) that crawled over them whilst they slept. Every morning they would hang any bedding they had over branches and beat as many of them out as possible, in order to secure a better nights' sleep tomorrow. It still makes my skin crawl to this day. I vividly recall the story of Uncle Peter stealing some fruit and the harsh punishments that followed. My grandmother also told us of a Japanese guard who had fallen asleep on duty and was hung upside down in the heat of the day – she was always clear that she felt sorry for the Japanese soldiers, as their punishments within ranks were far worse than those inflicted on the Prisoners of War. These horrific flashbacks were interspersed with stories of the colourful plays put on by the internees, the amazing quilts and stitching done under such risky conditions and the ingenious ways in which people, especially my Great Grandmother Morris, survived.

When asking the question 'Grandma, tell us again about the 'Camp',' you never quite knew which 'lens' the stories were going to be viewed through, whether they would bring faith or disappointment in humanity. Yet, there was a constant morbid curiosity that made my brother and I continue to ask the same question upon her visits and our trips to see her in Scotland.

When I was 21 and just finished university, the Japanese

Government gave my grandmother a small amount of money to 'compensate' her for the loss of those childhood years. That same year I was travelling to a family wedding in Australia and she asked if I would be her travelling companion en route. My grandmother wished to go back to Changi and visit family (the locals who had kept them alive in Camp by smuggling food through the fences) in Malaysia.

Seeing my grandmother back in Singapore and visiting the places she had grown up was an amazing and priceless experience. We visited the Changi Museum, where a photo of my grandmother and her family is displayed. It was taken on Changi beach, just before the invasion. It really hit home just how young they all were and how, just as in our recent pandemic, utterly unaware they were of how their life was about to change forever. During the visit, my grandmother and the family spoke in both English and Malay intermittently and some people we encountered were surprised when an elderly western-looking woman was furiously bartering in the market for food in their native tongue.

One evening, in Johor Bahru, while staying in a 'conference type' hotel where we felt slightly out of place without our pinstriped suits on, my grandmother's language skills did make me chuckle. We found ourselves in a lift filled with these suits who were intent on conducting a very heated debate once we joined them. The climb to the 11th floor was tedious, and the lift seemed to stop at every floor, whilst the debate seemed to get more intense and the number of suits did not seem to be dwindling. Finally our floor came, the doors opened and over her shoulder my grandmother said in a very loud voice 'Nona'– the doors slid shut as the jaws of the suits hit the floor. The debate had been about whether I was her daughter or granddaughter and there had been some heated deliberation about this. My grandmother had absorbed, listened and waited patiently for the right moment for maximum effect; maybe this had been a skill perfected in Camp?

The internment of prisoners during wars has impacted many future generations of families throughout history, through the stories told, the attachments formed or just because a glimpse of the worst part of humanity is seen through a personal lens and it is horrifying. These terrible experiences can also give us hope that by sharing stories of the past, we can learn from the story-tellers' resilience and make a better future for the world. Although not always comfortable to revisit, it is important that these stories are shared, heard and remembered.

EMMA MURRAY, APRIL 2023

Prologue

It's hard for me to imagine a lovelier childhood than the one my siblings and I shared in the Far East before the outbreak of the Second World War.

We lived in Johor Bahru, at the southern tip of the Malay Peninsula, just across the water from the island of Singapore. I was the second of my parents' four children. My big sister Mary was born in 1929. I followed in 1932. We had two younger brothers, Peter and George.

In those long-ago days before the Japanese occupation, we children felt we were growing up in a paradise. We only had to go into the garden to pluck mangoes and guavas straight from the tree. Holidays were spent at our hut on the golden sand at Changi Beach. We kept a monkey for a pet. When we weren't at school, life felt like one long adventure. We were surrounded by friends of all nationalities and there was always somebody to play with. Though officially we were British children, there's no doubt that to us Johor Bahru was 'home'.

So when war came to our region in late 1941, we did not

immediately try to leave, as many other British citizens in the region did. Why would we? Malaya, as we called it then, was where our lives were: our father's work, our house, our school, our friends. Of course we'd stay. Why would we want to be anywhere else? But to stay was a decision that would cost us three and a half years of freedom and change our lives forever, as our paradise was transformed into a hell.

OLGA HENDERSON

PART
ONE

Paradise

"One day, I went out to play, skipped into the forest and found three tiny tiger cubs sheltering in their den. I picked one of them up and took it back to show Mum"

1919 – 1941

I

MUM & DAD

My family's connection with the Far East began in 1919, when my parents arrived on the island of Singapore from different sides of the world.

My mother, Nora Smart, had grown up as part of a large family living on a farm in a village called Over near Swavesey in Cambridgeshire. Though she was a bright child, Mum had to leave school at 14 to work in her aunt's post office. After a couple of years there, she trained as a governess, but during the First World War, Mum worked in a munitions factory in Cambridge. It was hard but necessary work.

When the war was over, Mum moved to London, where she found a job as a nursery governess in Kensington. It was a good position and she might have stayed there but my mother was always adventurous and when she read about a vacancy for a 'pukka' governess in Malaya, she was immediately intrigued.

Mum attended an interview and was delighted to be chosen for the role – a four-year contract – living with a British expat family on a rubber plantation several hours' drive from Singapore.

Unfortunately, it wasn't simply a matter of jumping on the

next ship south-bound. Mum's new employers had previously been stung by a young woman who had taken money for her passage to Singapore but failed to turn up.

As a result of her predecessor's dishonesty, my mother was told that if she really wanted the job she would have to pay her own fare to get there.

Undaunted, she bought a ticket.

The voyage cost her £26 – equivalent to more than £1000 in today's money – plus a supplement of £1 to be able to take her sewing machine in the ship's hold. She wasn't going to travel without that.

After five weeks at sea – the most memorable part of which, according to Mum, was the day she won a competition for peeling an apple in one long strip – my mother arrived in Singapore. She found a room at the Raffles Hotel, where she would be staying for a further two weeks before her new employers were able to collect her for the onward journey.

These days Raffles is synonymous with five-star luxury but back then it was where all the new expat arrivals started out. On her very first night, Mum decided to eat in the hotel's restaurant. She was given a table to herself but after a short while, she was asked if she wouldn't mind sharing with another customer.

'It's very busy tonight,' said the handsome man who took the chair opposite.

Mum and her dining companion soon fell into conversation and not long after that, they fell in love. The handsome stranger was, of course, my father.

Dad was christened Hozack Morris but everyone called him Harry. His unusual first name was Dutch, and reflected the fact that his ancestors had sailed from the Netherlands to Ireland with the Prince of Orange back in the 17th century.

When my parents met, Dad had already been in the Far East for a while, though, like my mother, he was English by birth. He was born in Tintwistle, a charming little village in the High Peak district of Derbyshire, just north of Glossop. The tiny cottage where Dad grew up is still there today.

Tintwistle was a nice village but, like my mother, Dad wanted to see more of the world. His mother was a charlady and his father was a steel erector who had worked on the Blackpool Tower. Dad had inherited his father's talent for making things and was offered a place at university. Alas there was no money to enable Dad to take up that place, so he took an apprenticeship and trained to be a sanitary engineer instead.

One day at work, Dad had a need for a very particular type of screw. Since he couldn't find one, he had to invent one. He patented his design and with the money it generated, Dad emigrated to New Zealand. From there, he travelled to Australia where he bought two small opal mines in the country's east. The mines did well, and having socked away a bit of money, Dad decided to move to Singapore, with the intention of starting his own business on the island. With its long history as a trading settlement, Singapore seemed like the sort of place where an entrepreneur could thrive. While he waited for his opportunity, he worked for the Public Works Department on local infrastructure projects, building roads, hospitals and other official buildings.

That long-ago night at Raffles, my father knew at once that in Nora Smart he had found the woman he wanted to spend the rest of his life with. But of course my mother was contracted to work as a governess on that rubber plantation many hours away and, having spent all her hard-earned savings to get this far, she could not afford to give up the job and stay in Singapore for love.

After two weeks of getting to know each other, my parents had to say 'goodbye'. As they parted, my mother promised to write. And she did. For the next three years, Mum and Dad were avid penfriends.

At the end of those three years, Mum was tasked with accompanying her young charges from the plantation back to England. Having delivered the children to their new schools, she went to see her own family in the green-painted farmhouse that had been her childhood home. Upon arrival she discovered that her grandmother was gravely ill and it was decided that Mum would remain in England to nurse her.

Receiving the news that they were to be apart for even longer than expected, my father sent an engagement ring, made from a half-sovereign, with his next letter. Mum accepted his proposal and when her grandmother died, she sailed back to Singapore at the earliest opportunity.

Dad met Mum at the docks and they travelled onwards to Kuala Lumpur where my father had been working. Within days they were married in the city's Congregational Church.

2

TIGERS IN THE NIGHT

The newly-wed Mr and Mrs Morris were delighted to be together at last but there followed some very lean years. The Great Depression hit construction work hard. Fortunately, Dad had found employment building a mosque in Kuala Lumpur, so he and Mum set up home there and that's where my sister Mary was born.

When I followed two years later, my parents and Mary were living in Nassim Hill, Singapore, where Dad was working on the building of the central train station. Though Nassim Hill was a very nice area, Mum and Dad could only afford to rent the smallest bungalow. Money was tighter than ever, so much so that my parents couldn't find enough to pay for me to be born in Singapore's main hospital. My mother went instead to the 'Sepoy Lines', where an Indian soldiers' barracks was located, to give birth at the free hospital there.

Just as it is today, Singapore at that time was full of people of all nationalities trying to make their way. Just prior to my birth, my parents had befriended three Russian sisters, who had fled to the Far East in search of safety during the Bolshevik revolution. I was named Olga after one of those sisters. I don't have a second name and neither do any of my siblings. Our mother used to say 'I'm not going to give you a name that I have to go down the street and round the corner to say…' She liked to keep things simple.

My brother Peter arrived in June 1934. Little George came 18 months or so later. With a rapidly expanding number of mouths to feed and still hardly any work to be had in Singapore, Dad had no choice but to take a job 'up-country' again. This time he was contracted to work on the building of a psychiatric hospital in Tampoi, a village just outside Johor Bahru. We all went with him to live in a small wooden hut near the site of the asylum, as it was called in those days.

Our new home was a traditional 'attap' hut, made from the wood of the coconut tree and thatched with its large flat leaves. There was no running water or electricity. At night, the hut was lit with tiny oil lamps.

In Tampoi, we felt very close to nature. We kept a mynah bird, which we tried to teach to speak. There we also had our first pet monkey. At night, the little grey creature would climb into my bed to sleep alongside me. I loved to lay awake, cuddled up with him, watching out for animal eyes burning bright in the dark. There were wild animals everywhere. In the forest behind our hut there were wild goats, pigs, deer and strange possum-like creatures that used to get into the roof and make their homes there, keeping us awake by scratching about during the night. There were snakes too. You didn't ever go into the forest without making sure you had a stick to clear your path. It was at this time that we ended up having a pet python.

Sometimes Dad would take me to work with him on the hospital site. In the carpenters' shop there, I was trusted to pick up bent nails so that they could be straightened and used again. The men who worked in the shop, who were mostly Chinese, were very kind to me. Whenever they were sanding down a large piece of wood, they would save the long curly shavings and use them to make me funny wigs with stiff wooden waves.

One afternoon, I climbed up onto a shelf in a large linen cupboard the carpenters had been building and fell asleep there. When the carpenters found me they discovered, to their horror, that a python was curled up alongside me. Fortunately, the python had just eaten a young goat and wasn't interested in having me for his dinner.

The carpenters made a long box for the python and Dad and I took it home to show my siblings. We didn't know much about snakes and their eating habits and had no idea how long it would take for the python to digest its meal of young goat. After a couple of days, thinking that we ought to feed it, we put two live ducks into the box. The python was still not in the least bit interested in eating again and the ducks lived happily in the box – even laying eggs in there – for quite some time until Dad realised what was happening and let the ducks back out. He gave the python to the Chinese workers who had found it in the cupboard with me. We didn't try to keep a snake again.

Dad believed in treating all creatures with kindness. One particularly dry summer, when I was a bit older and we were living in Johor Bahru, he told us that if we found any newly hatched baby crocodiles while we were out playing, we should bring them back to the house and put them in the bathtub, which was filled with water. Dad said that, left to their own devices, the crocodiles might dehydrate and die. So for a while, we had a bathtub full of the snapping reptiles. I'm not sure what Mum thought of that! We fed them with meat that we held over the tub on sticks. As soon as they were able to jump for the meat, we knew they were big enough to be released back into the wild.

But the python and the crocodiles were not the most dangerous creatures I brought home...

There were tigers in the forest at Tampoi and on windy nights, when the attap walls of our house would flap open, we would sometimes see them, silently prowling through our garden, quite unafraid of any human.

One day, when I was still quite small, I went out to play, skipped into the forest and found three tiny tiger cubs sheltering in their den. I picked one of them up and took it back to our hut to show Mum.

'Look what I've got!' I said to her proudly. It was about the size of a six month old kitten and I thought it would make a good pet. 'Can we keep it?'

No, we could not. Mum was horrified, as was Dad. He told me that we must go and put the cub back exactly where I had found it at once. Hopefully we would get there before the mother tiger realised that one of her babies was missing. Thank goodness, we did. But that wasn't quite the end of the story.

Since the half-built hospital was the only building in the village with electricity, Mum used to take our laundry over there so that she could do her ironing in the light. Mum later told us that, on a couple of occasions, when she was walking back home from the hospital with my youngest brother George in his old-fashioned green Tan-Sad pram, at a certain point in the journey she noticed that an adult tiger was walking through the trees by the side of the road parallel to her.

The tiger didn't bother Mum. It just joined her for a certain portion of the walk, then peeled off into the depths of the forest as she got closer to home. Mum speculated that this tiger was the mother of the three cubs I had found in the den, accompanying Mum home as a way of thanking her for making sure that the cub I'd picked up was safely returned to her. The tiger was returning the favour, keeping Mum and George safe on their journey home.

3

FRUIT TREES AND
FLYING FOXES

We children would have been happy to stay in Tampoi forever, but when my sister Mary started school, that meant a
seven mile trip in each direction. When I reached school age
also, our mother insisted that we move back into town. So in
1936, Dad found us a house in Johor Bahru.

There's a certain stereotype that springs to mind when
people think of British expats in Singapore in the 1930s, but
my family definitely did not fit that mould. We were not part
of the privileged 'country club' set, with their big houses and
many servants. We'd moved out of an attap hut and our new
home was large enough for our needs but we did not have
teams of cooks and nannies to wait upon us.

Our mother preferred to look after and cook for us
children herself. Mum cooked a lot of what one might call
'English food' – we always had a roast lunch on a Sunday –
but we much preferred it when she adapted the recipes she'd
brought from home to the local ingredients. Though you'd
be hard pushed to find a potato in Johor Bahru, who cared
when there were so many wonderful local things to eat?

Mum would go to the market every day and got into the Malay habit of buying one's meat from the butcher then going to a special stall nearby to buy a mix of spices with which to prepare it. The spice man always knew what would work best with whichever cut Mum had bought. Mum took to cooking with the local vegetables too. We had aubergines, okra and lots of kang kung, a sort of spinach that grew in water.

There was always fresh fish, which I loved, however my brother Peter was not a fan. Whenever fish was on the menu, as soon as our mother wasn't looking, he would secretly pass chewed-up mouthfuls of the stuff to me, to hide in the pockets of my dress to be disposed of later. I must have felt very sorry for him to have put up with that!

As with all the local houses, in our Johor Bahru home we had a 'wet kitchen' and a 'dry' or 'clean kitchen'. The wet kitchen was where all the dirty work of food preparation took place, such as washing vegetables or gutting fish. The clean kitchen was where the cooking happened.

In the wet kitchen was a big 'Ali Baba' style urn that contained water, with a dipper hanging from it that we would use to wash ourselves when we came in from outdoors. We often got quite mucky during playtime, particularly if we had been down by the canal that ran through the village, past the hospital.

One of our favourite things to do was to head to the canal towards the end of the day when the town's water purification works emptied out. The waste water that flooded into the canal attracted fish by the hundreds and the fish attracted crabs, which we scooped up in a bucket. We would trap as many as we could – being careful not to get caught by the sharp tails of the king crabs – then take them back home to cook them in a kerosene tin over a fire. It was the freshest seafood imaginable and absolutely delicious.

Outside the wet kitchen there was always a row of 'terompah' – wooden-soled shoes, like clogs, with rubber straps – to keep our feet out of the mess. The rubber uppers were painted with different pictures so that we could recognise our own pair at once. Mine were painted with ducks. The terompah were designed so that we could rinse our feet without having to take the shoes off when we came in.

Other shoes were kept in a two-tier basket at the bottom of the stairs that led up to the back of the house. Whenever you pulled out a pair to wear, you'd shake them to make sure no scorpions had made their home inside. Likewise, you wanted to ensure you wouldn't encounter a blue centipede if you were putting your shoes on in a hurry. A bite from one of those would leave you feeling very sorry for yourself indeed with a foot the size of a balloon, or worse.

Our house had a verandah around the first floor. At one end of it, our father set up a hook from which he would hang huge bunches of bananas so that we could help ourselves whenever we liked. I especially loved the 'pisang mas', small sweet bananas barely bigger than your thumb (they are sometimes called 'ladies' fingers') that were even more delicious when dipped in batter and fried.

In our garden and up and down the street were many fruit trees that were always bursting with abundance. There were jambu trees, which sported pink skinned fruit shaped like a bell. Though the jambu fruit were also called 'Java apples', they actually tasted more like pears, with just a hint of cinnamon and rosewater. We'd look forward to those getting ripe. There was sweet mangosteen and durian too – the spiky-skinned fruit that famously reeks like rotting meat or sewage when you cut it open, but which tastes like heaven, if you can overcome the smell and get it as far as your mouth.

There was a guava orchard near our house. When the guavas ripened, they would attract flying foxes from miles around. These gigantic bats, which might have a wingspan of up to five feet across, would arrive in great flocks, covering the sky like huge black clouds as they flapped their way towards the fruit trees. The flying foxes fascinated and frightened us children in equal measure. Though their faces made them look like sweet little dogs with wings, they had sharp teeth and claws. You didn't want to tangle with a flying fox determined to get to a guava.

'Don't tease them!' our mother would warn us whenever they appeared.

4

PARTIES AND PRANKS

Johor Bahru was a very diverse town, where many of Singapore's essential workers lived, and we had friends of all nationalities, faiths and cultures. Respect for other people's religions was a given. Though there were no churches, the son of the Sultan of Johor Bahru, who was Muslim, had built a Sunday school for the local Christian children.

He told the local people, 'I've got lots of stables but not many horses.' So he cleaned out one of the unused stables, decorated it, put in some benches, and that was our Sunday school.

Every Sunday afternoon between two and three, the local Christian children would gather there to be taught by various local women including Mum. We'd be given little pieces of card printed with pictures of Jesus and bible verses to collect and learn.

As a family, we celebrated the festivals of every religion. We were often invited to our neighbours' family weddings. I loved making the traditional 'bunga telur', eggs dyed bright colours and embellished with artificial flowers, that were an essential part of any Malay wedding celebration.

At Hari Raya – which was what our Malayan friends

called Eid, the celebration at the end of the holy month of Ramadan – we would decorate our house, setting out oil lanterns on bamboo poles all along the path. It was so beautiful when they were lit. Hari Raya was a time for fire crackers too. I remember one year Dad bought us a whole string of crackers and tied them to a swing in the garden. When he lit the bottom cracker, they all went up in a crazy, swinging firework display.

Hari Raya was one of my favourite festivals. We would go from house to house, visiting friends to toast the season with sweet drinks coloured bright red with sarsaparilla. There were gifts too. In the lead up to the big day, Mum and I would knit cotton bootees and frilled bonnets for all the babies in the village. Everyone got new clothes for Hari Raya. I remember going next door and watching in awe as the men of the family appeared in their beautiful new sarongs, which were fastened with glittering pins that my friend Khatijah assured me were studded with real diamonds.

Since Dad did not have to work during Hari Raya, he would often lend his car to our Muslim neighbours so they could use it to visit relatives during the holiday. With no public transport, they'd have been unable to get there otherwise. Likewise, our Muslim and Hindu friends helped us to celebrate Christmas. Every year, Dad would buy three turkey eggs at the market in Singapore, which he would give to the hens to hatch, then we would fatten them up for Christmas dinner. On Christmas Day, we'd have the usual feast – as near to an old-fashioned English Christmas dinner as Mum could make it – then on Boxing Day, we'd throw a tea party for our neighbours with cake and ice-cream and games for the children. One year we had 54 guests at our Boxing Day table. My parents had bought a gift for every single one of them. It was such a great day.

I also had the privilege of taking part in some of the more solemn religious ceremonies in our neighbours' lives. When one of Dad's colleagues in Tampoi, a young Indian man, was killed in an accident, his traditional funeral pyre was built on the main road. I asked Dad if I could watch the cremation and Dad agreed to take me. Perhaps that wasn't the best idea. When the fire was lit, the heat of the flames made the tissues in the dead man's body contract so that it looked as though he was sitting up. I screamed and screamed and screamed. I thought he was alive! Dad had to quickly carry me away. Mum was furious and I didn't attend any more cremations after that.

Ours was a very close-knit community. We children were always in and out of each other's houses. We even carved a tunnel through the hibiscus hedge that separated our house from the house next door where my Malay friend Khatijah lived.

We shared our dolls and other toys but we didn't need much to have fun. We invented lots of games using whatever came to hand. We'd play at cooking, making concoctions from the hibiscus leaves that got all slimy when they were cut into small pieces. Another of our favourite games involved flipping flattened metal bottle tops into a hole we'd dug in the dirt. We called it 'ceper'. Each player would start with five bottle tops. The winner – the one who got most into the hole – would take the lot. Collecting bottle tops became something of a craze, with certain tops having more value than others, according to their rarity. Tops that came from other countries were the most highly prized. I still have an urge to save bottle tops whenever I see them.

In the afternoons, when it was too hot or wet to do much, Mum would sometimes read us stories in the shade. She also taught me, my siblings and all our friends how to knit – a skill which would come in very useful in later life. I learned how to sew clothes Malay-style too, thanks to Khatijah's mother, who showed me how to hold a piece of fabric tight across the top of my leg to make a good, even seam.

I loved to wear Malayan clothes. Wearing a sarong gave me so much more freedom than the European dresses we wore for Sunday best. I knew that whether I was sitting cross-legged on the ground or climbing a tree, I would be covered and protected from the sun and insect bites.

It wasn't all playtime. We did have chores. One of my favourites was sorting through the big bags of rice that were delivered to our house every couple of weeks. Mum would lay a big piece of coconut matting on the grass outside the house and pour the rice out onto it. Then my friends, my sister Mary and I would sit in a circle, sifting through the grains, discarding any that were still in their husks. It was an opportunity to chatter and laugh and sing together in all our different languages. A song that began 'teng teng' was one of our favourites. We sang it so often that one of the old ladies in the neighbourhood shouted 'for goodness' sake, shut up!'

Whenever we had the chance, we liked to be by the sea at our family beach hut in Changi. It was a very basic place, which had been built so that when the tide came in it would sweep through the hut and clean the floor, but we loved it there. Being by the sea always felt like a treat. Once, when we all had whooping cough, Dad rented a bigger house on the beach where we could recuperate. We were there for a month and no-one was allowed to visit in case we were contagious, but being by the water made being separated from our friends much more bearable.

When we were by the sea on holiday rather than recuperating, lots of friends would join us. We'd have delicious dinners thanks to the huge number of hawkers who plied their fresh wares on the sand.

We knew a Malayan family who lived near the beach who would go fishing at night and I managed to persuade Mum and Dad to let me go with them. As darkness fell, we went out in their sampan with a torch and a sieve. One of us would shine the torch on the water while another would use the sieve to scoop up all the tiny pink fish that were drawn to the surface by the light.

At other times, we took day trips up-country to the beautiful Kota Tinggi waterfalls, about 40 miles from Johor Bahru, where cool, fresh water tumbled down rocky ledges and formed lovely pools where we could splash about all day.

Back at home, we played games of hide and seek that took us all over the neighbourhood. Mum could usually tell where I was by looking for my shoes at the bottom of a tree.

I always took them off so that I could climb faster and higher than anyone else.

The guava orchard was an especially good spot to find a hiding place. On one occasion, during the flying fox season, I hid inside a hut where the farmers kept their tools, only for my sister Mary to block the hut door shut as a prank. When I didn't turn up at home in time for supper, every adult in the street turned out to look for me, but my naughty big sister kept quiet and I was stuck in that shed for half the night before she confessed to knowing exactly where I was. Generally, however, Mary was quite protective of me. She still is, more than 80 years on.

5

EVERYBODY'S CHILDREN

In our village, the bigger children always looked out for the younger children. I loved looking after babies. I would jump at any opportunity to help a new mother out.

Our father had a driver called Moktaya to take him to work. Sometimes, if he wasn't busy with Dad, Moktaya would fetch Mary home from school and let the rest of us children ride on the car's big mud guards for the last part of the journey.

Moktaya and his wife lived in a flat on the ground floor of our house. Tragedy struck when his wife died when their only daughter was just two years old. Devastated and desperate, Moktaya didn't know how he was going to be able to care for his toddler daughter and keep working, so he told our mother, 'I'll have to give her away.'

Our mother stepped in at once, telling him, 'You cannot give your child away. I will have her and look after her during the day and you can take over when you finish work.'

Mum was true to her word. After that, Moktaya's daughter, Pacheum, joined us every day. She became like a little sister to me. Though I was not much older than she was, I loved to carry her around, balancing her on my hip as I had seen my mother do with my younger brothers.

Next door, there was another baby – Keyno. I loved her too. Keyno hated going to sleep at night, so every evening I would volunteer to walk her up and down the long upstairs passageway in her family's house until she settled down. Everyone was happy to indulge my maternal instincts, until the local doctor – a dedicated Indian physician called Dr Mutatambe who made his rounds on a bicycle, and who had nursed us all through whooping cough and diphtheria – warned my mother that if she kept letting me carry babies around on my hip, I would probably grow up to be lop-sided. I didn't care. I was having a lovely time.

Our house in Johor Bahru was always full of children. Though she did not want servants, for a brief period, when she was unwell, Mum employed a Chinese woman who turned up on our doorstep one day, desperately seeking work so that she could provide for her own offspring – a toddler and a baby. The woman explained that her husband had been injured in a storm – he had been struck by lightning while standing under a tree and was very badly burned – and there was no money coming into their household while he convalesced.

Mum rightly wondered who would be looking after this woman's children while she helped Mum to look after us, but together they came to a workable solution. Our new amah would bring her children with her to work. They would play with me and my siblings while their mother was busy. And so our merry band of playmates grew again.

But there were other children in the neighbourhood who were much less lucky than me, my siblings and our friends.

Our house stood at the top of a steep, terraced garden that led down to a stream, which marked the boundary between our property and that of a Malay family who lived on the other side. From time to time, I would meet a little Malay girl down there. I would cross the stream to talk with her, out of sight of the adults, and we became friendly – playing games and weaving frangipani flowers into each other's hair. Gradually, I came to know her story. She wasn't the daughter of the people who owned the house where she lived, but an orphan girl they had taken in. Now she worked for them, looking after their new baby, though she could not have been more than six years old herself.

One day, after we had known each other for a while, I asked my mother if I could invite the little girl next door to my eighth birthday party. My mother agreed and I went round to the Malay family's house to deliver the invitation. I was overjoyed to hear that my little friend could be there. But the day of the party came and the little girl did not appear at the given time. I was very disappointed and, once the other guests had gone home, I took a piece of cake round to the Malay family's house, thinking that the little girl might have been unwell. This time, I was given a short shrift.

I discovered that my invitation had landed the girl in trouble. The Malay family did not want anyone to know that they were making such a young child work in their home. While I was enjoying my birthday party, she was punished for having become friendly with me. First she was beaten, then her employers rubbed powdered chilis into her eyes, after which she was forced to sit hungry and silent under the platform where the men of the family ate their meals.

Seeing my friend in a terrible state, I ran home to tell my father, who straight away went to the house and demanded that the Malay family hand the little girl over. Dad called the police and told them that a child was being kept as a slave. Malaya was under British Law at that time and such child labour was strictly illegal.

The scandal spread throughout the neighbourhood and eventually the Malay family was prosecuted for their ill-treatment of the orphan. I was called to court as a witness but I didn't get to go. Somehow on the day, Mary, my big sister, went in my place, though she hadn't been involved at all.

As a result of Dad's intervention and the subsequent court case, my little friend was adopted by a loving family. Years later, Mary bumped into her. By then my friend was grown-up, married and had children of her own.

6

CONVENT GIRLS

At the age of six years and three months, I started school, following my big sister to the Johor Bahru outpost of the Convent Of The Holy Infant Jesus. We weren't Catholic, or even particularly religious, though for a short while we did go to Sunday school. Dad's family was Irish Protestant. We attended the convent simply because all the girls who lived in our area went there. We'd hardly associated with another white family growing up. In my class were Indian girls, Chinese girls and Malay girls, as well as British expat children.

My friend Khatijah travelled with us to school each day. On our way, we picked up another friend, a Chinese girl called Ahong, whose mother had a shop in the village. Dad drove us before he went to work and to make sure we were on time, we had to be ready by eight on the dot. Dad was very firm about that. If you weren't standing by the car at eight o'clock sharp, you would be left behind.

Meeting Dad's strict deadline was easier said than done when getting ready involved taming my wild hair to meet the nuns' strict diktat that hair had to be 'contained'. I had a big mass of hair with tight springy curls that did exactly as they pleased, especially when it was humid. It always took Mum ages to get it all scraped back into a pony-tail, even using her trusty Mason and Pearson hairbrush.

My sister Mary was always worried that my hair, which took so long to tame, would make us late, so one day, to Mum's horror, Mary had Dad take her with him to his barber's shop, where she had her own beautiful hair chopped into a bob that needed nothing more than a quick brush through, making a point that she was not going to wait for me any longer. Mum was very upset.

Tidiness and cleanliness were very important at the convent school. Saturday mornings were spent preparing for the week ahead, cleaning our leather school shoes (having first made sure to check for scorpions) and putting 'blanco' on our plimsolls, to make sure they were sparkling white. Our uniforms, like our hair, had to be impeccable.

In the youngest classes, we were not taught by nuns but by Teacher Nora and Teacher Julie, who were Chinese and very pretty. They were both extremely kind and made going to school quite fun.

I quickly made friends with my new classmates. One of my favourites was Vivienne Koh, a Chinese girl who lived in a little house near the school. For my birthday one year, Vivienne gave me a gift that I would treasure. It was a miniature handbag that looked exactly like the handbags my mother carried. It made me feel very grown-up.

I became close to another girl, from an Indian family and I remember being invited to her house to play one afternoon. Outside the house was a terrace, covered with pots in which the family grew various herbs and spices. While I was looking at some berries that resembled small, red tomatoes, my friend's little brother told me, 'You can eat those.'

I popped one of the bright red berries straight into my mouth but quickly came to regret it. It wasn't a tomato but a Gundu Chili Pepper. After the shock of biting into that, I said I wouldn't visit my friend at her home again.

Shortly after I arrived at the convent, I had a bout of malaria that saw me put in hospital. All of us had malaria many times. I was only three on the first occasion. This second time I was also low on iron, which meant I needed iron tonic, which I hated. I hated being in hospital full stop – especially since my illness meant we had to cancel a family trip to the Cameron Highlands, the beautiful mountainous region to the north where many expats spent their holidays during the hottest part of the year. It was the second trip to the Cameron Highlands that we had to cut short – the first time because Mary fell off a see-saw and broke her arm.

Fed up one day, I decided to make my escape when I was next left alone in the ward. I told the nurse to draw the curtains as she left then, using them as cover, I slipped from my bed and crept out of the building, crossing the bitumen road into the hospital grounds. The hospital was on a hill. I got down that by rolling. I made further progress by walking in a storm drain, which was big enough for me to walk through unseen. Then, while I was walking along the side of the road that would take me back to our house, a taxi driver pulled his car up alongside me.

'Where are you going?' he asked.

I told him. I had hoped he would give me a lift back home, but the taxi driver knew exactly who I was (we were the only white family in our town until the Curtis family arrived with their six children in 1941) and he knew exactly where I was supposed to be. When I got into his car, he drove me straight back to the hospital, much to my disappointment.

After that, I had to attend the hospital on a regular basis to take my iron tonic under supervision. I would walk there – everyone walked everywhere – and Ahong's mother, whose grocery store was along my route, would always give me a sweet to eat when I passed her shop on my way back home. She knew how bad that iron tonic tasted. I was always very pleased to see her.

Though at the convent school we were taught in English, I could already speak Malay, Tamil and some Cantonese thanks to the friendships I'd built up in Johor Bahru. I was fluent in Malay and would accompany Mum to the market to act as interpreter in her exchanges with the market traders. To this day, I often still find it easier to find the word I'm after in Malay than in English and my sister and I will occasionally lapse into the multi-lingual parlance of our childhood when we're together.

7

EXPAT RULES

Mum was a very beautiful woman. I remember one day we were invited to a local wedding. Before we left for the ceremony, we all posed for a family photograph on the steps of the house. Mum was wearing a lovely pale mauve dress that she had made herself and a violet-coloured hat she'd bought to go with it. She looked so pretty that after he'd taken the photograph Dad told her, 'Go and change, Nora! You look much too nice!'

Dad was quite a jealous man, but perhaps he had good reason to worry that other men would find our mother attractive. When they were first married, Dad used to invite his friends over to the house to eat Mum's famous Sunday lunch. It was a very popular invitation, but Dad put a stop to the lunches when he realised that the men found Mum herself much more interesting than her roast potatoes.

As I've explained, my parents were not of the 'country club' set that typified British expats in the Far East, but Dad's work did bring them into contact with those people. Many of the expat men Dad met, who had come to the Far East without their families, also seemed to have left their morals back at home. Several of them took mistresses.

One such man was Mr Black.

Mr Black had a second family with his mistress, who was of part European and part Asian heritage – Eurasian was the term people used. Because of prejudice from both the European and Asian communities, it was hard for Eurasian women to find work, so becoming the mistress of an expat was, for some of them, the only way to survive. While Mr Black was in Singapore, he and his mistress lived as man and wife. He also openly acknowledged their daughters Eileen and Stella as his own, giving them both his surname.

Eileen, Stella and their mother became friends of my parents. I thought the beautiful Black sisters were so chic, dressed in their fashionable, wide-legged trousers, with their hair styled in perfect waves. I was especially fond of Eileen who was very creative. She was about 10 years older than I was and I hung on her every word. Eileen taught me how to make paper dolls and showed me how brightly-coloured toffee papers, saved and flattened, could be folded to make crinoline dresses and hats for my little mannequins.

Eileen eventually married an Australian man who was working as a junior botanist at the Botanical Gardens and became Mrs Addison. She had a baby right before the Japanese arrived – a daughter. Fortunately, her little family was among those that managed to escape before Singapore fell.

It was easy to see what attracted British expats to the Far East. The warm weather and the inexpensive yet luxurious lifestyle were so much more appealing than depression-era

England. In the years before the war, we certainly had a very lovely life. We had everything we needed in Johor Bahru, but Singapore itself was right on the doorstep for more cosmopolitan entertainment. Every Friday – which was a day off in our Muslim majority region – we would jump in Dad's car and cross the causeway.

My siblings and I loved going into the city. If our parents thought we could manage another pet, we would buy one at the city's market. My brothers had two pet bantam hens from there and once we came home with a beautiful little dog, a Pomeranian. She was extremely pretty, but none of us enjoyed the Saturday morning chore of combing through her fur to find ticks, of which there were an abundance in the forest around our home.

In those days, we earned our pocket money by collecting old newspapers and empty tins and bottles to trade with a hawker, who went from house to house collecting anything he in turn might be able to sell on to be recycled. The hawker was especially keen to take any bottles that had contained Singaporean light beer. Luckily for us, Dad liked to have that beer with his lunch. We children would lurk about the dining room so that we could snatch the bottles as soon as Dad had finished with them to add them to our cache. When the hawker arrived with his baskets suspended from a bamboo pole, he'd weigh what we'd gathered and make us an offer. It was never very much but to us children, it felt like riches.

With our pennies burning holes in our pockets, we'd go shopping for toys. We especially loved going to K Ba Ba, a Japanese shop, where Mary and I would buy packets of delicate paper flowers that would open up as if blooming when you put them in water. We would also shop at Little's or Whiteaway's, the city's department stores, for special outfits (Mum made our everyday clothes).

Whiteaway's was where we shopped for warm clothing for those two curtailed trips to the Cameron Highlands. I was delighted when Mum said we could choose what we wanted and I picked out a honey-coloured sweater with stripes and two tassels at the neck with pom-poms on their ends. I thought that sweater was wonderful with those pom-poms. While Mum, Mary and I shopped, George was transfixed by a display of waterproof watches, which included one that was dipped in a tank of water by a mechanical arm. It was difficult to get him to come away when we wanted to go to the next shop.

Our little brother George hated shopping but even he didn't mind a trip to Robinson's, another department store, where Jaga, the tall Sikh security guard, was always happy to let George sit and wait with him. While the rest of us went inside, Jaga would entertain George with games and jokes. The two of them became very good friends.

Sometimes, on a Friday, our parents would take us to a fun fair. There were three in Singapore at the time. We usually went to Happy World or New World. They were both huge, with rides, dance halls, shooting galleries and hundreds of stalls lit by Chinese lanterns that turned them into a fairy land.

There was entertainment on every level, from puppet

shows for the children to opera in all languages for the adults, and there were delicious things to eat on every corner. Ice-cream wasn't common in Singapore back then but you could get a sort of water-ice that was grated and coloured with different flavoured syrups – a bit like Slush Puppies. We children always wanted to stop by a stall that sold those and loved to watch the stallholders fill our glasses with a rainbow of colours.

There were many exotic things on sale at the fun fairs. I remember once walking through the stalls with my father and coming across a particular stand selling what I thought were big balloons. These balloons were in the shape of ladies – beautiful, life-sized dolls – with staring eyes and pouting lips.

As soon as I saw them, I knew I wanted one more than anything and pleaded, 'Please, Dad, I'd love to have one of those.'

To my disappointment, Dad shook his head and quickly hurried me on to another stall, where he tried to distract me with other much less interesting toys. It wasn't until many many years later that I realised that those voluminous balloon ladies were definitely not intended for children!

In the mid-30s, there were many Japanese people in Singapore, including the tailor my mother liked to use. Though I preferred to wear Malay clothes, Mum always tried to keep up with the latest European and American fashions. She found she couldn't keep Malay shoes, like the terompah, on her feet. She always wore canvas shoes by Bata. Likewise, she thought that European clothes suited her best.

Mum would take magazine pictures to show the tailor what she wanted and he would try to reproduce them. We liked joining Mum on her trips there. While she was being fitted for a new dress, we would sit in the tailor's cool waiting room, perched on silk-covered pouffes that looked like giant mushrooms.

Sometimes, the tailor's wife would offer us something to eat, which was a real treat. The tailor's children would come and join us too. We didn't speak Japanese and they didn't speak English, but we were able to understand each other perfectly well by talking in Malay. We enjoyed spending time with them and saw no reason why children, from all different races and religions, shouldn't be friends. The same went for the adults, or so we thought. Everyone seemed to rub along together and we all benefited from the many different international influences in food, fashion and entertainment.

Most trips to the city would end mid-afternoon. We'd head back over the causeway, perhaps stopping to visit a friend of Dad's who kept a honey bear as a pet. We all loved that bear, who was the cuddliest, fluffiest creature you have ever seen. But he was also mischievous. One afternoon, we turned up at Dad's friend's house for tea to find everywhere coated in soft, white feathers. Left alone for a couple of hours, the honey bear had ripped the stuffing out of all the soft furnishings he could get his claws into.

On other occasions, we would stay in Singapore until a little later into the evening. If the tailor's family hadn't already fed us, we would eat at the Latsa House. The food there was mostly based on beans, which I loved. Our father wasn't so keen and would sometimes eat elsewhere. Then perhaps we'd stay to watch a film at the newly built Cathay Cinema, which had air-conditioning that made all the difference in Singapore's hot and humid climate.

A visit to the Cathay Cinema was something very special indeed. I remember being enchanted by Shirley Temple in The Bluebird. None of my siblings wanted to see the film so I went into the cinema on my own while my parents and them went elsewhere. Though I was only eight, I wasn't afraid, since Dad had always encouraged us to be brave and independent. That day I was wearing a white dress, made from a fabric called 'tribalco', with a big bow on the back. I felt very adult as I walked into the cinema until I realised that my seat was at the very top of the auditorium. It was such a long way up. I wasn't sure I could make it up all those steps, which I had to take one at a time because they were so tall. I forced myself to keep going. Having been allowed such a grown-up privilege, I wasn't going to miss out.

The Bluebird was set in Germany during the Napoleonic wars and had much in common with The Wizard Of Oz. Shirley Temple played Mytyl, the spoiled daughter of a wood cutter. At the beginning of the story, Mytyl finds a beautiful bird in the forest which she refuses to give to her friend Angela, who is unwell, despite her parents' suggestion that it might cheer Angela up. The very next day, Mytyl's father is called up by the army.

Mytyl is then visited by a fairy, who sends her and her brother in search of the 'Bluebird of Happiness'. The search leads them into the past and the future, in a series of adventures – some fun and some frightening – accompanied by their dog and cat, whom the fairy has altered into human form. Just as in The Wizard of Oz, the film begins in black and white, but when the fairy transforms Mytyl's world, suddenly the film is in colour.

Awakening from her dream, Mytyl too is transformed into a kinder, more thoughtful child. At the end of the film the family learns that a truce has been declared and Mytyl's father no longer needs to go to war. In celebration, Mytyl gives the bird she found in the forest to Angela. It is, of course, the mythical Bluebird.

That old film has stayed in my memory all these years. Looking back I can see how, in its depictions of the Napoleonic army marching on Germany, it foreshadowed the occupation of Singapore. I must have thought about The Bluebird many times during those years in the camp as I longed for my own happily ever after, in which a truce might end the war and reunite my family too.

8

RUMBLINGS OF WAR

In September 1939, Adolf Hitler's forces invaded Poland and, as per the British government's promises, Britain and the Commonwealth joined France in declaring war on Germany. Of course we heard about it – over the radio and on the news bulletins we saw at the cinema before the start of the main feature – but it was hard to get too worried. Europe seemed so very far away. It was a five-week voyage from Singapore to England.

We were glad to be living somewhere so far beyond the reach of the Luftwaffe, with no rationing and no blackouts. Safe in our house in Johor Bahru, life for us carried on as normal. There were concerts, which we felt morally obliged to attend, to raise money for the people back home facing the threat of a German invasion, but we never even considered the possibility that we might one day face an invasion ourselves.

We certainly didn't think we needed to worry about the Japanese. During the First World War, the Japanese had been on the side of the Allies, against Germany. Yes, Japan had invaded China in 1937, but to many expats, that seemed like a local squabble that had nothing to do with us. We wouldn't get involved. In any case, Japan had recently been trounced by the Russians on the Manchurian-Mongolian border. What bother could such a small nation possibly be to established military powers such as Britain and the United States?

But it was not long before war crept closer to our door. After the occupation of France by the Germans on June 22nd 1940, the French territories in Asia were suddenly ripe for the picking. The Japanese stepped into the void, invading the northern part of French Indochina, with the intention of stopping imports. Immediately afterwards, Japan signed the Tripartite Pact with Germany and Italy. The signing of this defensive agreement, which was intended to deter the United States from entering the war in Europe, cemented Japan's place among the Axis powers.

Next the Japanese set their sights on the territories held by the Americans and the British. Then in July 1941, the United States placed an oil embargo on Japan, blocking some 88 percent of oil imports to the nation, and suddenly everything changed. The aim was to stimy Japan's attempts to expand its empire. How could Japan launch attacks without fuel? It seemed a good strategy but the result was only that Japan became more determined to break the blockade by annexing more territory.

Still, even with relations between the US, Britain and Japan deteriorating rapidly, most of our friends in Singapore and Johor Bahru were sanguine. Many expats were reassured by a parade which took place on the Singapore esplanade near Raffles Hotel that year, showcasing the military might of the British Empire. All the regiments stationed in Singapore took part. The parade included units from the Army, the Royal Navy and the Royal Air Force accompanied by the local police and staff from Singapore's military and civilian hospitals. Even Singapore's Boy Scouts and Girl Guides were included and the march was followed by a fly-past of RAF planes. As Singapore's governor, Sir Shenton Thomas, took the salute, it certainly looked as though the island was prepared for anything Japan might care to throw at it.

We did not go to see that parade. My father was not keen on the military. He didn't like the way some of the army men he'd met in the past had behaved. They acted as though they could do whatever they liked. Dad found them arrogant and rude, especially to the locals. What they didn't understand, when they insulted the locals within his hearing, was that Dad considered himself to have more in common with the Malay, Tamil and Chinese people he had lived and worked alongside for so long than with the men from his country of birth.

9

WAR COMES TO SINGAPORE

December 7th 1941 is a date that all Americans know from their history lessons as the day the Japanese bombed Pearl Harbor, the US naval base in Honolulu, Hawaii, bringing the United States into the war at last. That day, a Sunday, we went into Singapore as a family and had the same sort of jolly outing we always expected. We went to Robinson's and George, grumbling as usual that he hated shopping, was allowed to stay outside with his friend Jaga the security guard. When we picked George up at the end of our shopping spree, we said goodbye to Jaga with no idea of what might be coming next.

In the early hours that following morning, the Japanese launched their first bombing raid on Singapore where 17 Japanese G3M 'Nell' bombers, flying in from their bases in Indochina, unleashed terror on the city. It's said that the Japanese planes were detected while they were still a whole hour from Singapore, but the RAF did not scramble to intercept them because they feared that their own fighter planes might be fired upon by the Allied batteries in the darkness.

The RAF were not expecting to have to fly at night. It seemed no one was expecting a night time attack. They weren't really expecting any kind of airborne attack at all, wrongly believing that the Japanese did not have aircraft capable of making it so far from their territory. Though an air raid warning was sounded at four o'clock in the morning, Singapore's streets were not even in blackout when the Japanese arrived overhead half an hour later.

Though the Allies immediately opened fire, not a single enemy plane was brought down. The Japanese had cleverly split their planes into two groups, hoping to draw the Allied guns in the wrong direction. The ruse worked. The raid lasted for only half an hour, but it was long enough to wreak havoc.

First the local Royal Air Force bases at Seletar and Tengah were hit. Then several bombs were dropped on Raffles Place, right in the heart of the city, sending a clear signal that Singapore was not invulnerable after all.

We heard about the bombing on the radio. It felt strange, quite unreal, that the war had suddenly come so close. More than 700 people were injured and 61 were killed in that first raid. Our friend Jaga, the Robinson's security guard who had always been so kind to George, was among them.

Two days after that first attack on Singapore, Japan sank two British ships – the HMS Prince of Wales and HMS Repulse off Malaya.

The Japanese invasion of Burma began on the 14th December, Borneo on the 16th and the Netherlands East

Indies was their next target on the 20th. Then suddenly Hong Kong was in Japan's sights.

The attacks were all carefully coordinated to open up so many new fronts at once, that the Allies barely knew which way to turn.

From Britain, Prime Minister Churchill instructed British Major General Christopher Maltby, who was charged with defending Hong Kong, to fight to the death and expect no reinforcements. It seemed that Whitehall considered Hong Kong doomed before the fighting began. Maltby's job was to buy time for the rest of Britain's colonies in the Far East.

Even in the face of such a violent tragedy, some people in Singapore remained in a state of denial. It's perhaps no surprise, given that back in England, even Churchill had decided that the island was a natural fortress that the Japanese could never penetrate.

The war in Europe was keeping Whitehall more than busy enough without having to worry about Singapore. The Allies had recently sent some new troops over, but a British regiment trained on Salisbury Plain was in for a shock when faced with the heat and humidity of the Malay Peninsula. Even the change in food got the newly arrived soldiers down. Gun towers were built around the island, but many of them were fitted with guns that, according to rumours, could only move along a 45 degree angle and fired missiles that were only good for sinking ships, not for bringing down enemy planes or for land battles. Supposedly aeroplanes had also been delivered, but they arrived in parts, in boxes, and were never put together. Singapore was woefully unprepared for what was to come.

COUNTING PLANES

Soon the Japanese were flying sorties over Johor Bahru every day. At home in our garden we had a lovely large tree. It was a durian belanda, a type of durian with nodules on its fruit instead of spikes. As the fruit ripened, Mum would cover each one with a fabric sling to prevent animals from getting at them before we could.

The durian belanda was very easy to climb. In December of 1941, we would shimmy up it to get a closer look at the Japanese fighter planes flying over, taking bets on how many we would see. We were always pleased when we got the right number, but in retrospect, it should have been very worrying how many there were.

Dad was certainly concerned. He had recently finished building a new customs house down by the causeway between Singapore and Johor Bahru. Since then, he and his team had been set to work filling pot-holes in the streets on the main road from Singapore into Malaya, so that ambulances bringing injured soldiers back from the front line to further up the peninsula could get through. That road was heavily guarded as it was the only way in and out of Singapore. But the road repairs were a farce. While the government was sending Dad and his men to fill pot-holes, the Japanese were walking through the rubber plantations to either side of the road with no trouble at all, shooting anyone white they came across on the way.

As the fighting continued up-country, Dad took the situation into his own hands and built an air-raid shelter in our garden, where we and the neighbours could hide if the Japanese got any closer.

In late December 1941, school closed for the Christmas holidays. Despite the raids, it was a fairly jolly time. There were still concerts and plays to attend. High society people were still going to tea dances and having parties. Dan Hopkins and his band still played dance music until midnight at Raffles Hotel. The shops were still full of luxury goods. You could still eat very well in a restaurant, though perhaps not if you wanted fish, since Singapore's Japanese fishermen had been rounded up and interned. They were enemy aliens now.

We went to the Alhambra, Singapore's first air-conditioned theatre, to watch a pantomime. I remember that everywhere we went that Christmas we heard a song called 'Run Rabbit Run'. It became very popular among my friends, so popular that Mum was often seen to cover her ears and beg us, 'Would you please stop singing that tune!'

We celebrated the season as usual, inviting our friends and neighbours to the traditional party at our house on Boxing Day. Dad took the usual photograph of us standing outside in the garden wearing our Christmas party finery.

Me, Mary and our brothers posed with our friends Khatijah and Christine Curtis. I still have that photograph. My sister Mary looks unhappy to be in a paper hat. I know I was very annoyed to be dressed in a smaller version of the dress Mary was wearing, knowing that eventually hers would be handed down to me, so that I would be wearing the same plaid for years to come.

Then, between Christmas and New Year, we went to our hut on Changi Beach. We didn't stay long this time. The wait at customs at the causeway was much longer than expected and when we got to the beach, Mum was disappointed to see a different sort of people in our usual spot – mostly rowdy Allied soldiers on leave, determined to have a party while they could.

At Changi, the sand was edged with barbed wire and there were gun turrets everywhere but still the inevitable invasion seemed impossible to some; even though the adults now knew that Hong Kong had been captured on Christmas Day, and that both Allied military personnel and civilians there had been subjected to outrageous terror and cruelty. The Japanese may have signed up to the Geneva Convention, but their government had not ratified that signature and it was clear that they did not consider themselves bound to uphold any of the human rights of military personnel or civilians described therein.

Mum and Dad must have heard about those atrocities in the news but they kept it from us children, making plans in whispers when we were safely in bed and asleep.

The War Begins

"The air tasted acrid and the sky was black as night with smoke from burning buildings. The hours passed like years as we waited to get to the front of the queue to board a ship, any ship, that might take us out of this hell"

JANUARY – MARCH 1942

II

BACK TO SCHOOL, BUT NOT FOR LONG

At the beginning of January, Mary and I went back to the convent. Meanwhile, our brother Peter was off to school for the very first time. He was enrolled at the boy's school, which was the brother school to ours.

The term began in the usual way. On the first day, we prepared ourselves for the weeks ahead by neatly covering new school books with brown paper, filling ink-wells and sharing out supplies of pens, spare nibs and blotting paper. Everything seemed the same as ever. But we were just three weeks into the new term when our headmistress, Madame St Simon, gathered us together to tell us that the convent was closing down because of the war. It was the same story at the boys' school. Peter was disappointed. He had only just started. Little did any of us know that those three short weeks would come to represent the entirety of his formal education until he was 11 years old.

For the rest of us, being sent home from school seemed like the very best thing to have happened. We couldn't believe our luck, getting out of lessons again when we'd so recently had a holiday. Madame St Simon had not given us any reason to think that we needed to be worried about this new development.

But stuck at home with no lessons to go to, it wasn't long before we were all pretty fed-up. Mum had taught us and the neighbours' children to knit, so when the British Army sent out an unusual knitting request, our mother set us to work. We were asked to knit long thin strips, just eight stitches wide, to be used as belts for soldiers' pyjamas. The army had the pyjamas but they had been made without the cords that would hold the trousers up.

By late January, several of the expat families we knew had decided that it was time to leave for somewhere safer. Australia and South Africa were top destinations. We couldn't go. Our father was still being kept busy filling those potholes on the main road. Meanwhile, the little steam engine called 'Singapore' did overtime, picking up stranded soldiers up and down the peninsula.

I was bored stiff at home, so I jumped at the chance to join Dad on his journey to work. Sometimes Peter and George came too but for the most part I was the only one who volunteered to keep Dad company. Whereas previously I had left home at eight for school, now I had to be ready to leave the house at half past four in the morning. Dad's driver would pick us up and we would travel towards wherever Dad was working. We'd go as far as Dad and his colleagues considered safe, then he would drop me off at the nearest army camp.

My favourite was when he dropped us at the Sikh guards'

camp in time for a delicious breakfast of chapatis, cooked from scratch on hot stones heated in a charcoal pit at the side of the road. You never knew what they were going to pile on top of the chapatis but it was always delicious. I quickly learned to copy the way the men ate their spicy curries, balling the mixture up in rice and tossing it into my mouth so that I didn't get any of the hot chilli on my lips.

The Sikh engineers liked to spoil us children and we were delighted to let them. I would stay there until Dad finished that day's work. Straight after breakfast, the cooks began thinking about what to make for lunch and I hoped I would be there long enough to join them. While they were waiting for their instructions, the guards would play long games of something they called 'five stones'. They taught me how to play. Otherwise, I would just sit and watch the comings and goings until Dad returned to pick me up and take me home. Though he didn't ever tell me, sometimes his working day would be cut short because the Japanese were getting too close.

As January went on, more and more people were leaving. Having woken up to the reality that Singapore was not likely to hold out for much longer, the British Government was busy evacuating all their non-vital employees.

By now, I'm sure Mum and Dad were ready to go too but because my parents had come to Singapore of their own accord, rather than at the behest of any official body, we were considered independent. There was no place on an official evacuation ship for us.

Why did we not try harder to leave? Where would we go?

We fell through the gaps in the administration, I suppose. No one was looking out for us. We had to stay on. Besides, Dad still had work to do, repairing those potholes so the ambulances could bring ever more casualties back over the causeway.

12

'YOU'VE GOT HALF AN HOUR'

And so we remained in our house in Johor Bahru, watching the Japanese fighter planes fly over whenever they pleased, until one day towards the end of January 1942…

I remember it was just after lunch time. Dad was still sitting in his chair with his usual light beer and my siblings and I were playing with our pet guinea pigs when we heard the sound of a truck pulling up outside followed by hurried footsteps running up the stairs to our front door. Mum opened the door to find a breathless army man on the step who informed her, 'You've got half an hour to get your things together and be on my truck.'

The soldier told Mum and Dad that the Japanese were just 15 miles up the road now and the time had come for us all to be moved into Singapore, where we could be better protected. He said that once we were on his truck and safely across the causeway, the army would blow the crossing up in an attempt to slow down the Japanese advance.

'You're the last ones to be evacuated,' he said.

Mum and Dad didn't hesitate. The soldier had made it clear that time was of the essence. We children were put to work too. I remember that having just half an hour to grab what we wanted to take with us seemed almost like a game to me, Mary and our brothers. For us the highest priority items were our pets and our toys, of course. Peter wanted to take some beautiful German-made miniature cars. Little George wanted to take his train and his Mickey Mouse toy. I was determined to take my favourite doll – an American Betsy Wetsy.

Betsy Wetsy was my pride and joy. She was made of rubber. You could give her water from a bottle, that she would then 'wee' out into a nappy. I thought she was the best thing ever. Of course I couldn't leave her behind. I also wanted to take her little white wardrobe full of tiny clothes, my favourite Christmas present that year. It had a mirror on the front so that Betsy could admire her outfits.

While we were busy packing our toys, Mum and Dad were making much more practical decisions. They gathered up our clothes and as much tinned food and jars as they could carry – condensed milk, corned beef, Marmite, that sort of thing. They piled extra food into our arms too. Mum packed medical supplies and her sewing kit. But by far Mum's cleverest decision was to pack our family photograph album. Though she could not have known it at the time, those photographs would be very precious to us in the years to come. With the album and everything else loaded onto the truck, we were finally ready. Moktaya was to follow behind in the car.

I had wanted to take my pet cat with me but she wasn't allowed to join us, as we were going across the causeway and – ridiculous though it seemed with all the bombing going on – all the usual customs rules were still in place. Domestic animals could only cross with clearance from a vet and there was no time for that. The guinea pigs had to stay behind too. The family dog couldn't come for the same reason, though he ran behind the truck for as long as he could. It was heartbreaking to watch him finally give up and trot back to the house. We could only hope our Malay neighbours, who weren't being evacuated that day, would take pity on him. Though that was unlikely given that, due to their religion, the Malays didn't like to touch dogs at all – especially if the dogs were wet. Years later, we'd learn that elsewhere expat families had taken the difficult decision to have their pets put down rather than leave them to fend for themselves.

That afternoon, we headed at top speed for the causeway where a small group of soldiers was waiting for us. When we got there, Dad jumped down from the truck to have a word with the army engineers tasked with detonating the bridge. He could see at a glance that they had laid the explosives in the wrong place but no one seemed to want to listen to him, though he knew that causeway better than anyone.

They were young soldiers, still quite green, and only concerned with obeying their senior officers' orders. Though their officers were equally unfamiliar with the local geography and the tides, the soldiers assumed their superiors must know better than this experienced engineer.

Giving up on trying to persuade the soldiers to try another approach, Dad climbed back onto the truck and we drove on into Singapore. Exactly as planned, the army blew up the bridge the moment we were safely out of range.

What next? We wondered as we watched Johor Bahru disappear into the distance through the smoke of the explosion. Where were we going to live now?

13

UNCLE TOM

Our father had arranged for us to stay with Uncle Tom. The man we called Uncle Tom was not a relative of ours but he was a great friend to our parents. A bachelor in his forties, very tall and thin, he had often spent Christmas at our house, along with his beautiful Eurasian mistress, whom we called Auntie Amy.

Uncle Tom was the manager of a pineapple factory in the city. He had a house on the Maxwell Road. It was not a large place and he already shared it with his housekeeper – an elderly Malay woman, who had looked after him for years – but somehow Uncle Tom promised to make room for us all.

It was a novelty to be crammed into Uncle Tom's two-bedroomed cottage and, in the beginning, we were happy to treat it as an adventure. But there were signs everywhere that things were bad and getting worse. Singapore had suffered a great deal of bomb damage. The two shops on Uncle Tom's street were closed down and boarded up, as were many other businesses in town.

Later that day, as we unpacked the luggage we'd put together so hurriedly, my sister Mary realised that she did not have her new watch with her. The watch had been a special birthday present and she was most upset that she couldn't find it. Mum spoke to a local man who made his living as a palm reader – many people believed in such things in those days – and asked him what he thought had become of it. He told Mum that the watch was still in the house in Johor Bahru, but that it was hidden underneath something. That was enough for Mary, who insisted on going back to the house the following day.

Dad was willing to make the trip because there were several other things at the house that we needed, which had been left behind in our half-hour scramble to be ready for the evacuation. Dad took Mary with him. Mary was wrapped up in a mattress in the back of the car to protect her from flying shrapnel.

In theory, Dad and Mary should not have been able to get back across the causeway, but of course Dad knew that wouldn't be an issue. He'd been right about the army engineers. They had placed their explosives in the wrong place. At low tide, the causeway was still easily crossed on foot and with the aid of just a couple of planks Dad was even able to drive the car over. It was at once both comical and ominous, how easy it was for Dad and Mary to get back to Johor Bahru. The Japanese infantry, who were largely travelling on foot and – ridiculous as it seemed to us then – on bicycles, would not have a problem with the causeway at all.

Dad and Mary got to the house without encountering any trouble. While Dad loaded up the car with more tinned food and other vital possessions – including Peter's precious bantam hens – Mary searched her bedroom. She searched high and low and was almost ready to give up when she decided to check her wardrobe one more time and there, under the lining paper at the bottom, was her missing watch. The fortune teller turned out to have been right. Goodness knows how the watch had ended up under the paper but there it was. Wrapped up in the mattress again, Mary brought her precious treasure back to Uncle Tom's house.

With everything that Dad and Mary had retrieved on this trip added to the things we had gathered in that mad half hour before we were evacuated on the army truck, it was getting a bit cramped inside Uncle Tom's, so it was decided that some of our things would have to live outside, under the external staircase. Among the things which had to be put there were Peter's chickens and my doll's wardrobe. This combination unintentionally caused much amusement, as the chickens would catch sight of themselves in the mirror on the toy wardrobe's door and fly into a rage, thinking two other chickens – strangers – were muscling in on their patch. Watching the bantams fighting their imaginary enemies was a welcome distraction.

We'd been used to being able to wander all over the neighbourhood in Johor Bahru, playing our games and visiting friends, but now we had to stay close to home at all times. We were not supposed to leave Uncle Tom's yard, though of course we children did, sneaking out through the back gate to watch the comings and goings on the main road. We needed to be out in the fresh air. Uncle Tom's house was so small that there wasn't enough room for all of us to play indoors. If you were sitting in a chair and got up for any reason, someone else would quickly steal your place. It caused plenty of sibling squabbles. We were like wild animals suddenly expected to live in a farmyard. But at least we were safe, though we had to sleep on the floor with our mattresses on top of us as protection from shrapnel from the Japanese bombs which were now falling on the city every night.

14

OUR FRIENDS IN THE ARMY

Those weeks we spent at Uncle Tom's might have been a frightening time but as children, we just went along with it. Far worse than the fear of being bombed was the feeling of hunger. We all loved Uncle Tom's smiling housekeeper, who in better times had always been ready with a cuddle and a helping of the delicious jelly she made with the blue flowers of a creeper that grew on the patio.

She did her best to keep us well fed now but there was very little for her to cook with. Though our parents had brought all the provisions they could carry, it wasn't long before we were running low on fresh food with nowhere open where we could easily buy more.

Unfortunately for my brother Peter, as supplies got tighter it was decided that we would have to eat one of his chickens. We did the bird proper justice, eating every part of it over the course of four days.

But worse was to come.

Within a few days of arriving in the city, we had no running water in the house.

Knowing that there were many Allied troops on the island, the Japanese planned to bring Singapore to its knees by cutting off the fresh water supply. On an island, we were surrounded by water on all sides but with the Japanese having taken control of the reservoirs, there was barely a drop to drink.

Luckily, help was at hand on that front. Uncle Tom's house was one of a number of houses that were set in a horseshoe shape around a central, circular green, in the middle of which a recently-arrived British Army regiment had set up camp.

We became friendly with the soldiers, sometimes offering our services as translators when they wanted to talk to the locals in Malay or Cantonese. The soldiers had put up a tarpaulin to catch rainwater, which they shared with us. The weather was very wet that year so there was always plenty of rain to catch. They also gave us several large tins of peaches. We gladly ate the fruit and mixed the juice with the rainwater to make it taste more palatable.

We washed in the rain too. Mum told us that rainwater was the best water for rinsing our hair in any case, and would send us outside with a bar of soap whenever there was a heavy shower (which was probably far too often as far as we children were concerned. We were quite enjoying the opportunity to let the strict rules about looking clean and tidy drop for a while).

Having the soldiers on the green made us feel safe, though the bombs continued to fall and the news coming out of the rest of the Far East was very bad indeed.

As we huddled beneath our mattresses at night, I hugged my Betsy Wetsy tight and assured her that everything would be back to normal soon.

15

'YOU'RE NOT OFFICIAL'

The British, the Australians, the Canadians and Americans were still evacuating as many people as they could and as the fighting intensified Dad decided that at last it was time for us to go too. We gathered together our most precious belongings and made for Keppel Harbour, in the hope of getting a boat out of the city. We'd heard that it might still be possible to get to Australia.

The Japanese were bombing the city and there was fighting on the streets as we started out on our dangerous journey. So that we wouldn't run into any trouble, our mother cleverly took us down into the storm drains that ran beneath the concrete paths. She thought we would be safer there, but it was a horrendous experience and one I have never forgotten, much as I would like to. It was very different from the time I had used the storm drains to escape from the hospital. The blood from people dying in the streets above was running down into the drains, where it mixed with the rainwater. In some places the muddy red soup was up to our knees. It was our first real experience of the horror into which we were about to descend.

When we made it to the harbour, we joined a long queue

of people with exactly the same idea as us. It was time to abandon the city. While Japanese bombs rained down, we were jostled and pushed out of the way by expats desperate to get away. The air tasted acrid and the sky was black as night with smoke from burning buildings. The hours passed like years as we waited to get to the front of the queue to board a ship, any ship, that might take us out of this hell.

When we were finally on the gangplank, we dared to think we might at last be on our way. But then our mother handed over our papers to the man who was overseeing the boarding chaos. He gave them just a cursory look before telling Mum, quite bluntly, 'you're not official'. As far as he was concerned, because we hadn't come to Singapore under the aegis of the British Government, he had no responsibility for us. Though we were all British citizens, we were not on that day's evacuation list and he would not be letting us board. It did not matter how Mum pleaded. 'Rules,' said the jobsworth on the gangplank. 'Are rules.'

It seems ridiculous now to think that at such a moment, with the Japanese bearing down on us and bombs exploding all around, that whether or not we could be helped to escape came down to having the right paperwork. It should have been obvious that we'd be prime targets for the enemy if we stayed. But we had encountered someone who was going to stick to the regulations despite our plight. That's what some people were like. There are still people like that now, who won't bend a rule even if someone's life depends on it. Children's lives.

Defeated, our mother accepted that we were not going to

be sailing anywhere that day. As we trudged back down the gangplank, she tried to reassure us, telling us in as cheerful a tone as she could muster, 'It doesn't matter, children. We'll go back to Maxwell Road. We're probably safer where we are in any case.'

We had no choice but to go back to Uncle Tom's house and hope that the Japanese didn't find us there.

It turned out that Mum was not entirely wrong about us being safer at Uncle Tom's house than on an evacuation boat. Moments later, as we watched a ship carrying people we knew leaving the harbour, destined for what we hoped was freedom and safety, we saw it hit by a Japanese missile. The ship quickly began to list and the passengers who'd thought they had been rescued found themselves tipped into the water. We realised then that the Japanese fighter pilots were just waiting until the ships were out of the protective area around the harbour to fire upon them. Those ships were sitting ducks.

Many years later, I learned that of the 46 ships involved in the evacuation of Singapore, only six ever made it to their final destination. In some ways, those of us who were left behind did turn out to be the lucky ones. Many of the people who boarded those ships died in the following days, as the Japanese navy picked them off one by one. Thousands drowned. Others made it to dry land only to be killed on the beach. Still others survived the sea and the danger of landing in Japanese-controlled territory, only to end up being rounded up and put in camps along with the rest of us.

When we got back to Maxwell Road that night, the army regiment that had been camped on the green was getting ready to go to the front line. As they passed us, marching with their heads held high towards unknown horrors, one of the soldiers stopped me and admired the ribbon I was wearing in my hair. The ribbon was red, white and blue.

'Do you need that?' he asked me. 'Can I have it?'

I didn't hesitate. I took it off and gave it to him straight away, hoping that it might bring both of us luck.

The soldiers had left their kit on the green when they set off to fight that day. They didn't think for one moment that they might not come back. Neither did I.

16

THE FALL OF SINGAPORE

We were holding out as best we could, but eventually the inevitable happened. Churchill's island fortress was no such thing. Blowing up the causeway had made no difference whatsoever. While Japanese bombers continued their assault with barely any opposition (most of those Allied Planes never did make it out of their boxes), the Japanese infantry simply marched or swam across the Straits of Johor and were soon stalking Singapore's streets in their strange, cloven-toed rubber boots.

As the battle reached its climax, Churchill sent orders, demanding that Singapore fight to the last. He wrote, 'There must at this stage be no thought of saving the troops or sparing the population. The battle must be fought to the bitter end at all costs... Commanders and senior officers should die with their troops. The honour of the British Empire and of the British Army is at stake. I rely on you to show no weakness or mercy in any form.'

Certainly, the Japanese were showing no weakness or mercy as they bestrode the island, killing military personnel and civilians alike. They even attacked the city's hospitals. The Red Cross, a symbol of the protection international law provides the wounded and those who help them, meant nothing.

Some of the worst atrocities were seen at Singapore's British Military Hospital, where the Japanese ignored the entreaties of a British officer wearing the red cross and carrying a white flag, who pleaded with them to spare his medical team, and went from room to room bayoneting patients, doctors and orderlies alike. As many as 280 were killed in the most horrific ways imaginable. The rest were taken as prisoners of war.

While all this was going on, we could do nothing but stay inside Uncle Tom's house and wait and hope we would survive the night. We huddled together and did our best to stay calm.

Our prayers were not answered. My soldier friend, who marched into the fray with my ribbon tied to his rucksack, did not return triumphant. None of his colleagues came back either. Instead, on February 15th 1942, Lt General Arthur Percival, General Commanding Officer Malaya, surrendered Singapore to the Japanese.

The horrible ceremony took place at 5.15pm in the island's Ford Factory on Bukit Timah Hill. There Percival signed the demand for unconditional surrender in the presence of Japan's General Yamashita.

Some 80,000 British, Australian, Indian and other local troops were taken prisoner.

Churchill called it the worst disaster in British Military history. It had taken the Japanese only 70 days from first landing in Malaya to occupying the region's jewel in the crown. Singapore had fallen.

17

THE 'SOOK CHING'

The Battle of Singapore had turned the city into a hell, but with the surrender, the brutality of the Japanese towards civilians had only just begun. Suddenly Japanese soldiers were all over the city. The British Army regiment that had helped us to survive without mains water and with little food was gone. Captured or killed? We did not know.

We stayed indoors as much as we could, but there was no choice but to venture out from time to time to find something, anything, to eat and to keep from going mad. I remember how one day I crept out of the house to see what was happening on the main road when I saw an act of such cruelty that it has stayed with me for more than 80 years. If I close my eyes, I can still see it in horrible detail.

Two Japanese soldiers were talking on the green outside Uncle Tom's house. A young Indian boy, whom I vaguely knew from playing outside before the Fall, passed nearby the soldiers on an errand. As he got close, they grabbed hold of him and accused him of eavesdropping on their conversation. They decided he was spying. The little boy protested his innocence. In any case, why would he understand Japanese? But the soldiers showed no mercy. One of them took out a knife and, without a moment's hesitation, cut off one of the poor boy's ears. The soldier was smiling as he did it.

I ran home, faster than I had ever run, and told Mum what I'd just seen. Though of course my parents were appalled and angry, there was nothing they could say or do to make a difference. There was nothing any of us could say or do anymore, lest we ended up missing more than just our ears. A couple of hours later, 20 civilian men were marched onto the green, blindfolded and killed by a firing squad.

This became a regular occurrence in a systematic mass killing that became known as the 'Sook Ching' – Chinese for 'purge by cleansing'. Now that they were in charge, the Japanese were officially rounding up all the 'anti-Japanese' elements on the island, though in truth they weren't being that discriminating. There's still no clear consensus on how many people died in the Sook Ching of 1942, but estimates vary between 25 and 50 thousand. The bloodshed seemed endless from where we were hiding. Every day another group of men – mostly Singaporean Chinese – would be marched onto the green and shot. I saw it happen more than once. I don't know why I stayed there, watching the killings from Uncle Tom's front gate. I think perhaps the shock of everything I'd witnessed so far had made me numb. I've heard of other children, who ended up in the camps, finding themselves unable to look away from scenes of the most awful cruelty. There was something in the horror I was witnessing that held me transfixed, unable to look away.

The green, which had once been a place for playtime, picnics and parties, was now nothing but an execution site.

The blood of the dead and dying ran into the gulley at the back of Uncle Tom's house. We children were no longer allowed into the front yard at all. We hardly dared look out of the windows. And all the time, we wondered when it would be our turn to face the guns. The Allied soldiers were all gone now. We were on our own.

18

ENEMY ALIENS

What happened next was the Japanese classified us as 'enemy aliens'. Sir Shenton Thomas, the newly deposed governor of the Straits Settlements, was forced to make a public announcement, requiring all Europeans to present themselves for registration. Shortly afterwards, two Japanese soldiers came to Uncle Tom's house to make sure that my family obeyed this new diktat. We were directed to the offices of the new Japanese administration, in what had formerly been Singapore's law courts and city hall.

We were ordered to walk there and told that we could only take what we could carry: one suitcase per person maximum. Sensing that something bad was afoot, Mum immediately pulled on a number of dresses and filled all her many pockets with food – marmite and condensed milk – her sewing kit and aspirins. I took my Betsy Wetsy but not her wardrobe. Peter had his cars. George clung on to his train and his Mickey Mouse toy. Mum made us all put on our school shoes, which would turn out to be a very good idea, when we were faced with a long walk through streets filled with shrapnel and rubble.

Once we were ready, we said 'goodbye' to Uncle Tom (for

some reason he hadn't been called to register with us that day) and his lovely housekeeper. It didn't feel like a permanent sort of farewell. We thought we would probably be back.

Perhaps we should have known. We found ourselves walking through a city that was unrecognisable as the place we'd so enjoyed visiting at weekends when we still lived in Johor Bahru. There was bomb damage everywhere. The walls of buildings were pock-marked by gunshot from street battles. Though the guns were silent for the moment, the air was filled with dust and smoke.

Japanese army cars, painted with the symbol of the Rising Sun, buzzed through the wreckage. Japanese soldiers sneered at us from beneath their caps as we passed. There was no doubt who Singapore belonged to now. The Japanese flag flew from every flag post.

It was horrible to see so many enemy soldiers on the streets but far worse was seeing the dead bodies of the Allied troops and civilians who had been caught in the fighting. We saw pale arms sticking up from the rubble as though they were waving for help. We saw feet without legs and bodies without heads. Our parents tried to keep us from looking too closely at such things. 'Just keep going,' they told us. It was all we could do.

I remember that at one point in our journey that day we had to cross a bridge. On every post of the bridge was a severed head, mounted on a spike. I recoiled in fright as I realised we would have to pass right through that macabre, medieval horror. I can still see some of the dead men's faces in my mind's eye now, decades later. That particular memory never fades. Those men. Sons, brothers, fathers. Who were they? I've often wondered. Who did they leave behind?

As we got nearer to the law court, we were joined by other Europeans heading to be registered by the new administration. The adults were grim-faced, doing their best to stay calm for the children who wanted only to stop walking, sit down and have something to eat. It must have been hard for the grown-ups not to lose control.

When we reached the doors of the law court, a Japanese soldier barked at us, telling us to bow. Of course we did exactly that, having learned by now that when a Japanese soldier issued an order, no matter how petty it seemed, you'd better obey it. Then we stood in line to be registered. There were soldiers everywhere, watching us, waiting for the slightest excuse to pull someone out of the queue and give them a beating. We tried not to make eye contact as we waited for our turn at the desk.

When we got to the front, the Japanese officer in charge asked for our papers. Dad handed them over. As the officer shuffled through them, he made a comment about whisky – I'm not sure what or why – to which my father replied with some pleasantry. Dad's comment, though perfectly innocuous, was met with a furious response. The officer immediately put his hand to his sword and shouted, 'If you speak to me again like that, I'll cut your head off.' Given all that we had seen happen on the green the past few days, we had no reason to think he was joking. My sister, my brothers and I cowered behind our parents. My father quickly apologised and we all stayed silent from then on, eyes ahead, focussed on nothing lest the officer make good his threat. Was this how life was going to be from now on?

After registration, we were told to go outside and wait in the Padang for further instructions. Padang is the Malay word for field and that's exactly what this place was. It was an open playing field in the downtown area of Singapore, overlooking the sea.

In happier times, it had been used for playing cricket. Now it was a mustering point for us 'enemy aliens'. Hundreds were already there and still more arrived every minute.

We were forced to wait in the Padang for hours, through the heat of the day, with no shade, no food, no water and no toilets (we just had to squat where we were while Mum shielded us with her skirt), as we waited to find out what the Japanese were going to do with us next.

It quickly became clear that the Japanese had not expected to find themselves having to deal with so many prisoners. The Japanese martial code – the Way of the Warrior – did not allow for something so shameful as surrender. The Japanese had assumed that the Allied soldiers would feel the same way, but they had already filled the city's barracks in Changi, built to house 5,000, with 50,000 Allied military prisoners. They were in no way prepared to deal with so many civilian prisoners on top of that number, especially not so many women and children. Where were they going to put us?

For the moment we were just glad to be together: Dad, Mum and the four of us children. Having Dad with us we felt somewhat protected from the strutting Japanese troops.

Dad always knew what to do. But that feeling of safety in his presence wouldn't last long.

After many hours on that cricket pitch, we were told we were going to march to Katong, six miles away from the Padang on the island's eastern coast. That news was bad enough – a six-mile hike – but as we got ready to move, the Japanese separated the men from the rest of us. We wished our father 'goodbye' and prayed that it wouldn't be for too long.

19

KATONG

Six miles is a long way to walk in the tropical heat, especially when you're a child. Mary, Peter and I straggled along, carrying what we could and trying not to complain. Mum had to carry my younger brother George, who was too small to make the journey on foot. We walked separately from the men. Armed guards escorted us all the way, barking at the slowest among us to pick up the pace and delivering the odd whack with a rifle butt to those who continued to lag behind.

After hours of trudging through a hellscape, we arrived at our destination. We knew something of Katong from before the war. In more peaceful times, it was a pretty market town. There was a beautiful beach there and it was home to a famous tuberculosis hospital run by Doctor Elliot. Oh, but how it had changed. Many of the buildings had been bombed. Those that hadn't been bombed had been looted.

When we got there, we found that hundreds of men, women and children were already crammed into the buildings – including a number of run-down hotels and a couple of cinemas – which the Japanese had ear-marked for the purpose of housing us until a more permanent solution could be found. The men were squeezed into the Picture

Palace while the women and children were sent to the Sea View, a former guest house. Others who had arrived there before us had already taken the bedrooms, so we found ourselves stuck in the foyer with only a single reclining chair between the five of us. Mary and I sat on the floor, while Mum took the chair and held the boys on her knees.

There was nowhere to lay down in comfort, neither was there anything to eat. When my brother Peter started to whimper, Mum did her best to soothe him, wary that his crying might upset the other women around us or, worse, enrage the Japanese soldiers in charge. We'd already seen what they could do when they were angry. 'Don't cry,' she told him. 'We're not all crying.' But I could understand why Peter was finding it hard not to sob. I wanted to cry too. We were all so tired and hungry.

Hearing Peter's distress, a kind woman whom we'd never met before did her best to help, giving him a cream cracker and half a sardine to take the edge off his hunger. The rest of us had nothing. We lay down to sleep that night on the hard floor of the foyer with our stomachs growling and our feet aching and sore.

When we woke the following morning, having slept fitfully, we had just a few blissful post-dream moments of confusion, before we looked at the room around us and remembered where and who we now were. We were in captivity. Stuck in the overcrowded foyer of a hotel where once jolly holiday-makers had relaxed after a day on the beach, we were prisoners with no idea of our fate.

20

THE BEST AND
THE WORST

The Japanese had collected hundreds of Europeans from all over the city by now. More and more prisoners arrived in Katong by the hour, making what was already a bad situation even more uncomfortable. Little did we know that we would be at the Sea View Guest House for a fortnight, crammed into that stuffy foyer with a chair for a bed.

It was very unsettling, not knowing what was happening in the world outside or what had become of Dad. The armed guards made sure we could not mix with the men or get any messages to them.

We were astonished at how harshly the Japanese guards treated certain of those among us. We had grown up in a culture in which men always treated women with kindness. Likewise, the elderly were always treated with respect. That did not seem to be the case as far as the Japanese guards were concerned. They lashed out indiscriminately and at the slightest provocation. Didn't matter whether the person they hit was a woman, a grandparent or a child.

What little hope we'd had that we would soon be released

from the guest house and repatriated started to wane. Food was in short supply. There were no real washing facilities. The toilets, which were not designed to be used by so many people, soon became blocked and filthy. As people grew hungrier and dirtier, tempers frayed and we quickly discovered that while war might bring out the best in some people, in others it brings out the worst, encouraging bad behaviour. And the people who behaved especially badly weren't always the ones you'd expect.

Among the women at Katong, there were two Christian missionaries – Mrs Weekly and Mrs Thornley – who were given permission by the Japanese to go back into the city to collect people's belongings in their car. It was surprising that they still had petrol, which was hard to come by. Since our internment had happened so quickly, most of the people caught up in it had not had time to properly prepare and they'd come away without clothing, bedding or food. The missionaries asked my mother if there was anything that she'd like them to pick up.

When we'd been ordered to leave Uncle Tom's house to register at the old law courts, Mum had cleverly put on several dresses – one on top of the other – and made us children carry things like cotton thread. Mum was a talented needlewoman and had an idea that she might need the tools of her trade. She had also brought with her soap, which would become very valuable indeed.

Thanks to Mum's quick thinking, we had come to Katong with more than most, but Mum still asked the missionaries if they could fetch us some extra clothes and any food items they might find since it was clear that we were in for a longer stay as prisoners of the Japanese than we had expected. Plus, Mum was having to look out for five of us.

We looked forward to the missionaries' return, hoping for a change of clothes and perhaps something nice to eat, but when the missionaries came from their trip into the city, they told us that they had found nothing at Uncle Tom's. 'The house must have been ransacked,' they claimed.

In the moment, we accepted their explanation, thinking that Uncle Tom must have been taken prisoner too by now, leaving the house undefended, except for his Malay house-keeper who would not have been able to stop determined looters. However, a few days later we noticed that other women at Katong were suddenly wearing clothes that we knew for certain had once belonged to our mother.

While Mum would not have begrudged any of those other women something they really needed, she was very upset to think that the missionaries had lied to her and taken the decision to share her personal things with strangers out of her hands.

The clothes were emblematic of something much bigger for Mum. She had had a very religious upbringing in a strict Christian sect. I remember her telling us that on Saturday evenings, the family would prepare for the Sabbath by covering every mirror in the house and preparing all the food they would need for the following day.

Mum's last task each Saturday was to prepare her grand-mother's special church cloak, which had an intricate collar with dozens of pleats that had to be steam-ironed one by one. Sundays were entirely devoted to God, with nothing but bible reading and prayer all day long.

The cult members only ever wore black and certainly never wore make-up. The younger members' behaviour was always closely monitored. Mum often told the story of how, one day, she'd ridden her bicycle from Over, where she lived, to Swavesey. Her route took her down a steep hill. To reach top speed, she had put her feet up on the handlebars and lost her balance. In the course of doing so, she lost a button. Though she searched high and low, she couldn't find it and got into terrible trouble when she had to admit what had happened.

No wonder Mum had jumped at the chance to take that governess job overseas. In Singapore, Mum had found freedom. She had been able to wear whatever she wanted and enjoyed having beautiful clothes, which couldn't have been more different from the plain black garments she had to wear as a child. Among her most precious possessions was a beautiful Spanish shawl, embroidered with colourful flowers, that had been a gift from our father when they were first married. Mum loved that shawl and so of course she recognised the moment she saw it wrapped around the shoulders of another woman. It hurt her especially badly to see something that had meant so much to her in someone else's possession. She knew that Mrs Weekly and Mrs Thornley could only have found it at Uncle Tom's house. Mum didn't feel very Christian towards the missionaries after that.

PART
THREE

Changi Days

*"Changi Jail had not been built with comfort or
peace in mind. Everywhere you looked was concrete.
Only concrete or steel."*

MARCH 1942 – MAY 1944

21

THE ROAD TO CHANGI JAIL

On March 8th 1942, after two weeks at the Sea View, we were on the move again. We were told to muster at dawn. It was before dawn, really, since the Japanese had changed Singapore's time zone to correspond with that of Tokyo. Japan had previously always been one hour ahead.

For three hours that Sunday morning, we had to stand in line and wait for our instructions. By the time the orders came, it was almost 10 o'clock and the sun was already high in the sky. The coolest part of the morning had been wasted and we began another march in tremendous heat.

We did not know where we were going or how long it would take us to get there. Had we known we would be marching for 11 miles that day, I think many of the women who had been crammed into the guest house would have given up before they started.

The Japanese soldiers transported some of our heavy baggage on a lorry while we prisoners set out on foot. Our procession included the very elderly, the pregnant and even small children who had to walk until they could go no further, at which point they were allowed to get on the truck too. The rest of us had to keep going.

Mum carried George in her arms again. We kept most of our luggage with us. No one really trusted that the luggage they put onto the lorry would make it to wherever it was we were heading. The Japanese would just take what they wanted, we were sure. One woman insisted on hanging onto an enormous carpet, certain that it would be stolen en route if she didn't hold onto it tightly.

Our march comprised women and children only. Though we would later discover that the civilian men had also been moved that day, I never did find out how. Did they have to march as we did? It seemed more likely that they were transported in trucks, being a greater risk to their Japanese captors than we could ever hope to be, after two weeks of no sleep and hardly anything to eat. Still, we were escorted all the way by guards with guns, as though we were dangerous criminals.

Mary and I walked at the head of the line with the other children. Peter teamed up with some young friends he had made in Katong. We wanted to be at the front because we were eager to find out where we were going and to bag the first beds if there were any to be had. Our late arrival at Katong had shown us that when it came to getting a good place to sleep, it was a matter of first come, first served. We were even slightly excited at the thought of a new adventure, thinking that wherever we were going had to be better than where we'd been.

For most of the march, George stayed with Mum, who

carried him for as long as she could. When Mum had to take a rest, Mary stepped in to help and gave our little brother a piggy-back at the front with us. But George cried for our mother whenever he wasn't with her. Mary kept him going as best she could, promising that we'd meet up with Mum at the end of the walk, but his constant questions – 'where's Mummy? Where's Mummy now? Will we see Mummy in a minute?' – were difficult to take.

We were lucky to have our mother with us on that march. Several children at Katong had arrived there without their parents. Some of them didn't know what had become of their families, who had likely died in February's fighting. Among them was a little Eurasian boy called Gordon, who was about the same age as George – just four or five years old. He wasn't sure. Poor Gordon was completely alone. He couldn't give the adults at Katong any information about his parents. He didn't even know his own surname. Feeling great pity for the child, our friend Muriel Shorthouse, who was married to a soldier, decided to take Gordon under her wing.

Muriel knew what it was like to be without any love and support in the world. A Eurasian woman, she had grown up in a desperately poor family and been sold into prostitution at the age of 17. Though she was pregnant at the time we were taken prisoner by the Japanese and had enough to worry about on her own account – where was she going to give birth? – she cleverly registered Gordon as 'Gordon Shorthouse', claiming him as her son, so that he could stay with her on the march to Changi and beyond. Not knowing when Gordon was born, she gave him the same birth date as my brother Peter.

It was a terrible journey. We were all much hungrier and weaker than when we had arrived at Katong – and we'd been tired and hungry enough then. Though it was the dry season, the heat was extreme and the sun beat down upon our heads without mercy. We fashioned makeshift headgear from whatever we could find – cardboard, towels, old newspapers. Some people even wore lampshades to protect their heads from the sun. I remember one middle-aged woman who wore a wonderful hat covered in silk flowers for the whole journey, determined to keep up appearances in these most terrible of times.

Several women had made trolleys, using abandoned pram and bicycle parts found in Katong, upon which they carried small children and bulky things like bedclothes. To begin with, we had a bicycle, from which we could hang our bags, but we were told we had to leave that behind. Peter and George had to give up their toy cars too. There were more important things to take.

It was hard for the smaller children to keep pace all day. We were all wearing flip-flops that stuck to the melting bitumen surface of the road as we walked. The hot tar burned and blistered our feet. It was far from being a pleasurable promenade.

As our strange procession straggled on, some of the locals who lined the route jeered and cheered – they thought we were getting our just deserts – but others were concerned.

They didn't see us as the enemy, but as friends and neighbours, women and children, fellow human beings being treated without dignity or care.

Our mother must have been suffocatingly hot that day. She was wearing five of the dresses she'd rescued from Uncle Tom's – every pocket stuffed with tins, pins and aspirins – and was carrying a big bag as well as our little brother. She was obviously struggling.

As we got closer to our destination, a Chinese woman, who had been watching us walk by, spotted Mum and decided to help. The woman had a guyung – a little tin that you dipped into a large jar of cool water – from which she offered my mother and brother George a drink. It was a kind gesture that was to cost her dearly. Spotting the interaction, a Japanese guard swiftly whipped the Chinese woman to the ground. We had to keep on walking, to the sound of our good Samaritan being beaten for trying to help Mum and George. We don't even know if she survived the beating. All we could do was keep marching without looking back or risk being beaten ourselves. Keeping our heads in such a situation was of paramount importance. It was a matter of survival now.

Such brutal acts as the beating of that poor Chinese woman were designed to send a clear message to the locals that any attempt to help European internees could be punishable by death. The Japanese were keen to convert the local population to their cause. During the fight for Singapore, they had dropped propaganda leaflets as well as bombs, in an attempt to rally the Asian population of the island. They had painted us – the Europeans – as a monstrous colonising hoard. The propaganda doubtless echoed the thoughts and feelings of many locals, but the Chinese Singaporeans remembered only too well the way the Japanese had treated their countrymen during the Sino-Japanese War. They had no reason to believe that the Japanese would suddenly start to see the Chinese as equal partners. There was no trust there. Especially after the Sook Ching.

Propaganda was very important to the Japanese. All the time we were walking, Japanese staff cars whizzed by, occasionally stopping so that the well-fed officers sitting in the back could photograph us, as though we were some sort of carnival parade.

Those pictures inevitably ended up in Japanese newspapers, where the camps would be described as 'Civil Internment Centres' where internees lived 'in harmony with each other.'

Finally, we arrived at our destination. So exhausted were we from the walk, it was a while before we realised we were standing in front of the white walls of Changi Jail, formerly home to Singapore's most notorious criminals.

While we were counted in through the huge gates, as more Japanese guards trained guns on us from the prison's watchtowers, some of the women began to sing. They chose 'There'll always be an England.' It was a small but important act of defiance that raised our morale and helped us to take those final steps.

Years later, we'd learn that the men who were already being

held in a separate part of the prison, heard the women's voices and for just a few moments they found their spirits raised too.

22

OUR NEW HOME

And so we arrived at Changi Jail, the civilian prison next to the Changi barracks where the Japanese were already holding the several thousand Allied military prisoners they'd taken after the surrender. When the Japanese took over the island, they had opened the gates of the jail to let the men who had been imprisoned there free, making space for an altogether different calibre of inmates.

The jail, like the barracks, was relatively new. It opened its gates for the first time in 1936. Built to house the Malay Peninsula's most notorious criminals, it was the perfect prison, designed to be absolutely inescapable. The three cell blocks and associated administrative buildings were hidden behind double walls. The outer set, painted white, was studded with watch-towers that were now occupied by Japanese guards. The inner set was 14 feet high. Outside the walls were 88 acres of farmland where prisoners could be set to work.

What would it be like, we wondered. We were not a family that knew much about prisons. We certainly hadn't had occasion to visit this one before. Mum made sure to be with us as we were counted inside the walls. As our names were checked off, we were funnelled into a long, empty passage, at the end of which were a set of steel doors. It was a relief to take off our sandals and walk on the cool, concrete floors, but I think we knew that once we were through those doors, for many of us there would be no getting out again.

We were told to go to E-block to see a doctor who had been interned along with us and was registering new arrivals. Dr Margaret Smallwood was an Australian. She tried to put us at ease and we hoped that once we had been registered, we would be fed. But there was no food to be had. Not yet.

After two weeks in the guest house foyer, taking it in turns to sit on a single chair, we had also hoped that we might get a bed at last but it was obvious from the start that our new accommodation was no big upgrade on the conditions at Katong.

The former prison had been built to house 700 prisoners (though it had been overcrowded from the moment it first came into use). Now it was home to 3,000 civilians. As more and more women and children piled in, we began to wonder if we would have to sleep standing up.

While we milled about, tired and longing for something nice to eat or somewhere soft to sleep, Dr Smallwood and a handful of other women – also doctors – who had informally elected themselves leaders of our rag-tag band, tried to impose some order and make sure that everyone got what they needed, to the extent that was possible.

But first we were gathered in front of the jail's new Japanese commandant for an address, during which he made clear the discipline and behaviour which was expected of us all. He was careful never to use the word 'prisoner'. We were not prisoners but internees, he said, being held for our own safety. That seemed a pretty hollow distinction to us.

After the address, Dr Smallwood and her team set about showing us where we were going to be sleeping that night.

E-block was a large concrete building. At one end was a curve that had been earmarked as a hospital. The doctors had found two screens, left behind from when the camp was still a prison, and put them up there to give patients some privacy.

In the middle of the block was a dining hall with a concrete table running down the centre, flanked by two painfully uncomfortable concrete benches, designed so they couldn't be moved. Presumably, that precaution had been taken to stop the jail's original inmates from throwing furniture at each other. That was where we would be eating.

There were rooms on the ground floor that must once have been offices, and cells on the floor above. We started out sleeping in what was called the 'carpenters' shop'. It had been some kind of workshop. It was a large square room with wire netting all around it and overhead. On our first night, we were each allocated a place on the floor where we lay down like sardines.

Changi Jail had not been built with comfort or peace in mind. Everywhere you looked was concrete. Only concrete or steel. The acoustics of the place were terrible. The slightest sound reverberated off and was magnified by the metal bars and concrete walls. You can imagine what it was like with Japanese guards shouting and children crying through the night. Some of the women who weren't mothers themselves were not very kind about the noise the babies made. There was just no escape from the sound.

Shortly after we arrived, our family was given a room on the ground floor of E-block in one of the old offices. It was not an enormous room but it had to accommodate me, Mum, Mary, George and Peter, and a Eurasian woman whom we hadn't previously met. This stranger had been put in with us to make up numbers since Dr Smallwood and the others had calculated that to fit everyone in, each room had to have at least six occupants.

As we arranged our meagre belongings in our stark new home, our new companion introduced herself. She told us that, while she was half Chinese, she had an English husband, which was why she had been rounded up. She said that her name was Elise but it wasn't long before we discovered that her birthday was April 1st and after that everybody called her April.

23

ANYTHING YOU LIKE AS LONG AS IT'S RICE

Over the next few days, a routine was established, revolving around meals in the concrete dining room, sitting on the hard concrete benches at the hard concrete table.

The meals on our side of the jail were cooked on makeshift stoves that the women had to build themselves using bricks. There was very little equipment – just an old wok found in the prison grounds that we'd had to clean the rust off with stones and a single wooden spoon – and the food was often spoiled, since very few of the women had any experience of cooking rice in volume. For many of the white women, cooks and other household servants had been part of the expat experience. They didn't know the first thing about food preparation. But we could not afford to waste food through bad cooking. Not a scrap.

After a lot of petitioning, the women who had taken on the mantle of leadership in the camp persuaded the Japanese officers that it would make more sense for our food to be prepared in the men's side of the prison where they had a proper kitchen block – one that had been designed with mass catering in mind. In the men's camp at that time, there were also a number of trained chefs amongst the Canadian naval men brought in after they survived the sinking of an evacuation ship. They were used to cooking for hundreds of people at a time. Perhaps realising that allowing the professionals next door to cook for the women would mean that less food was ruined and wasted, the Japanese officers agreed.

The 'menu' was pretty much the same every day. Breakfast consisted of a cup of tea, sweetened with condensed milk if we were lucky. We generally weren't. For lunch and dinner, we had rice boiled until it had the texture of glue. Or tapioca, cooked in a similar style. On high days and holidays we might get half a banana or a piece of gula batu, a sort of rock sugar. On other days, the rice might be flavoured with a morsel of fish, so rotten that we wondered whether it would have been better not to have it at all. Meals were a fraught time. We were always looking out to see whether other people had more than us.

The food was brought in from the men's camp in huge round tubs that we knew had been used for a very different purpose before the occupation. They had originally been used as receptacles for the city's night-soil, collecting human waste house to house. Though they had obviously been cleaned and boiled and cleaned a hundred times before they came to be used to carry our rice and tapioca, it was still strange to see our dinner being transported in them. It was hard to shake the memory of what had gone in there before! I wonder now if the Japanese had repurposed those tubs deliberately, to remind us of our diminished status in their eyes. But in those early days, the more the Japanese tried to humiliate us, the more determined the adult women in the camp became that we prisoners should hang on to those values that we'd been taught in the outside world. That meant queuing nicely for the food despite knowing it would be a disappointment when it finally arrived. Table manners were important. We children only ever went into the dining room with an adult and we were expected to behave when we were there.

Treats were in short supply. There was, however, for a brief period at the prison, a Japanese commandant who had been married to an American woman, with whom he had two daughters. Perhaps imagining his own children in our place, he took pity on us. He managed to get us some raisins. It was heaven to have something different for once. He also got hold of some palm oil to add to the rice, which he hoped would go some way to make up for the lack of green vegetables. We were grateful to have something with the water rice, which we called Booboo, but unfortunately it gave us all diarrhoea.

24

A DIFFERENT KIND
OF EDUCATION

The adults did their best to keep us children amused and happy. Left to our own devices, we could make our own fun but as we got used to camp life, the grown-ups became worried that we were missing out on an education. My little brother Peter, who had spent just three weeks at school, could only remember learning how to sing a song that began 'Good morning, good morning. How do you do? I'm very well thank you. How are you?' He sang it all the time and it drove Mum mad. Mum did her best to teach Peter how to read, but Mary and I needed more direction.

Among the women in the camp were six doctors, natural leaders, who took it in turns to act as camp commandant. They liaised with the Japanese officers on our behalf. Our first official commandant was Dr Eleanor Hopkins. Her husband, also a doctor, was in the men's camp.

There were some teachers in the camp too, though none that I recognised from the convent in Johor Bahru. Our teachers there had been Chinese and thus escaped the round-up. But one of the teachers who did end up in the camp was Mrs Milne, former head of education in Malaya. At the request of the mothers, a few weeks after we were interned, she took it upon herself to try to set up a makeshift school.

It was a risky business, asking the Japanese if we might have some, or any, school supplies. The Japanese commandant could have punished Mrs Milne for even daring to ask. But years later, I heard that Mrs Milne and our internee camp commandant Dr Hopkins overcame our Japanese captors' reluctance to allow education by explaining that there was a great deal of enthusiasm among the children for learning the Japanese language (we'd already had to learn the Japanese national anthem). Thus the Japanese commandant was flattered into providing us with a number of slates to write upon. He was also persuaded that Mrs Milne should be allowed to write back to Britain to get a copy of the curriculum for the school certificate – the equivalent of modern GCSEs.

Mrs Milne was an interesting woman. She never wore a dress but was always dressed in khaki trousers. A woman in such masculine attire was unusual at the time. She taught us spelling and arithmetic. There were bible stories too. We learned all the books of the bible by heart. We were taught poetry in the same way. Mrs Milne also taught us the names of all the plants that grew in the land around E-block.

Some of the older children, including my sister Mary, were taught by a younger woman called Freddy Bloom, a New Yorker. Freddy was only recently married to Phillip, a military doctor who was being kept in Changi barracks.

Though she had been working as a journalist before the occupation, Freddy Bloom was a natural teacher.

In some internment camps, the makeshift schools became quite elaborate. In one camp on the Chinese mainland where the entire teaching faculty of a university had been imprisoned, school was taken very seriously indeed, with some of the older children receiving such a comprehensive education that they were able to go straight to university after liberation, skipping the usual entrance exams. In another camp, the internees even set up their own medical school, catching frogs and rats for lessons in dissection.

I was only nine years old – almost ten – when we started our prison camp lessons and I remember receiving a less vigorous education but one that meant I could somewhat keep up with the children in the world outside.

To some of the adults, it might have seemed like a bother, having to arrange school lessons for the youngsters when there were so many other practical – and far more immediate – concerns than teaching very young children to read or preparing interned teenagers for the school certificate. But those lessons were probably as important to the parents in the camp as they were to the children, giving the mothers a few valuable hours of peace and quiet each day while we were being kept busy. I can also see now that our camp school was vital too as a means of reminding ourselves that outside the prison walls was a world that we might one day rejoin.

25

THE ROSE GARDEN

Our life in Changi wasn't all about school work. To the side of E Block was an open space we called the 'Rose Garden'. At certain times during the day we were allowed out there to practise acrobatics and run races – boys versus girls. We invented games like 'drop the hanky', which was riotous fun. We would all stand in a circle facing inwards, while the person who was 'it' walked around the outside and dropped a handkerchief behind another player, who would then have to race around the circle to tag the person who was 'it' before he or she stole the empty place. We also played 'five stones' and a variation on the bottle top game we'd invented in Johor Bahru. If anyone could get hold of a piece of string or wool, we could amuse ourselves for hours by playing 'cat's cradle'.

The rose garden was partitioned off, with us on one side and prisoners from the men's camp next door working the land on the other. The hastily-constructed dividing wall was made of cloth and wire netting and had a little ledge that we would use as a barre for ballet lessons. We had tap-dancing lessons too, in the long prison corridor. It would have been the perfect place to practise, had we had the right shoes. As it was, we could only imagine the sound our frantic footwork would make.

We didn't have many books in camp – few people had thought to bring piles of books when they were required to register at the law court – but for a while we did have coloured pencils and chalk. We drew hopscotch boards on the concrete pavements around the building. The plain endpapers of those books we did have were soon ripped out and used to fashion cigarettes for those women who smoked.

One day I found just enough paper to make a paper doll and a wardrobe full of clothes for her, as Eileen Black had once shown me how. I made her a real fashion-plate with long, curly blonde hair and pink lipstick. That paper doll became one of my most treasured possessions, particularly after it became clear that Betsy Wetsy was rapidly deteriorating in the heat and humidity.

Betsy Wetsy was an early casualty of life in the camp. Because she was made of rubber, the heat and humidity made her sticky. When we were at home in Johor Bahru, I would dust her with talcum powder and was able to keep her from getting tacky like that. In camp, there was no talc to spare and so she started to fall to bits when I played with her. Her rubber skin would just stick to my fingers and come away in patches. I remember asking Mum to help me save her with tears in my eyes, but there was nothing to be done. Poor old Betsy Wetsy.

It might seem strange, but despite our circumstances, we were still able to have a lot of fun in Changi in those early days. Though the adults must have found it hard living in such close proximity with each other, when they had been used to large houses and a certain degree of privacy and comfort, for us children it was wonderful to be living with our peers. There was always someone to talk to. It was heaven to have playmates on tap, whatever the wider picture. Children are very good at adapting to the worst.

Our friendships were very important. We made some good friends in camp. My brother Peter became very protective of a little girl called Joan Davidson, whom he treated like a little sister. I was outgoing and knew everyone and everyone knew me.

One of my best friends was Ozzie Hancock, whose mother was Portuguese. Ozzie had two sisters – Olive and Clarence, who liked to be called Gebu. Also in our group was Eileen Harris, who was a year older than me.

Eileen's mum was Indian and her father was Welsh. Before the occupation, Eileen's father had, ironically, worked as a guard in the very prison where we were now being held.

When the Japanese took over, for a while Eileen, her three siblings and their mother, who was pregnant, had been able to evade capture, passing themselves off as Malay. But when Eileen's mother gave birth, the new baby was very white. It caused people to ask questions about the father, which led the Japanese authorities to find out that Eileen's father was a British citizen.

After that, the whole family was rounded up and brought to Changi to be interned with the rest of us. That was terrible news for Eileen, but having her and Ozzie around definitely made my life in prison more bearable.

26

THE BIRTHDAY GIRL

Three weeks after we arrived at Changi, I celebrated my 10th birthday and it was decided that I should have a party. A prison is hardly a place to throw a birthday bash, but with the help of several of the women interned with us, who donated what they could to the project, Mum made the day as special as it could be.

One of the women found some white organza, which Mum made into a pretty party dress. When she realised that the fabric was see-through and needed a petticoat, Mum quickly stitched one together using empty rice bags. Someone else made me a birthday cake out of rice. Then, while we were getting ready for the big moment, we heard a shout and a woman called Mrs Mulvany came charging along the hall to where I was waiting to make my big entrance.

'Look what I've got for the birthday girl,' she called out.

She opened her hand to show me a piece of blue ribbon. After so many weeks in captivity, that scrap of ribbon looked as precious as a string of pearls.

'Turn around,' said Mrs Mulvany.

She wound the ribbon around my waist. Dressed in my

scavenged white party frock, with that beautiful blue ribbon as a sash, I had one of the most memorable birthdays ever.

Mrs Mulvany was very good at bringing a party together. On Sundays, the Japanese allowed one of two vicars, who were being held in the men's camp next door, to come through the barbed wire to celebrate mass with the women.

Shortly after my birthday, Mrs Mulvany persuaded the Japanese that we should be allowed to celebrate Easter with a tea party after the service. There wasn't much in the way of Easter food – there was certainly no lamb – but together with her friends, Mrs Mulvany created a beautiful table for us to gather around. At another time she put on a fashion show, for which many of the women made beautiful outfits from what little they had. One woman even made beads from the coir matting. Such things kept our spirits up.

We put on several concerts in the camp in those early months. In the carpenters' shop was a platform made of planks that became our make-shift stage. From time to time, the men from the camp next door were allowed to come through the barbed wire to take part in a show or watch one of ours.

I remember being in a play about a chocolate factory. The kind Japanese commandant – the one with the American wife – somehow managed to get us some real chocolate at one point. Each Saturday morning, we children would line up and he would give us each a cube, telling us it was the last chocolate bar in Singapore. Until eventually, we really were eating the last chocolate bar in Singapore and he couldn't get any more.

For another entertainment I wore my birthday frock and Mrs Mulvany's blue ribbon sash to sing a song about a lady in a blue dress, which might have been 'Alice Blue Gown', a song from the popular 1919 Broadway musical 'Irene'. People were always singing. One of the most popular songs in the camp was 'Begin the Beguine', which my sister Mary says became 'like a hymn' to her. It's hard to hear it now without thinking of those Changi days.

27

A DAY AT THE BEACH

These early days of birthday parties and fashion shows gave us a false sense of how life would be as POWs. Inevitably, conditions at Changi got worse. We had water to wash in twice a day (in showers that were completely open so that any guard passing by could stop to watch – in fact, they placed a chair there) but even with the help of the kind commandant who brought us raisins and chocolate when he could, food was so scarce that we were soon living on our own bodies and starting to waste away.

Disease was everywhere. We had typhoid in the camp. Fortunately, I never caught that. All the children were vaccinated against it by Dr Smallwood and Dr Elliot. Though the Japanese were very keen that we should have them, camp vaccinations were an awful experience. There was only one needle. It was plunged in boiling water between uses to keep it sterile but having been used on dozens of people it hardly had a point. You can probably imagine how horrible it is to be stuck with a blunt needle. The vaccine was diluted to go round and afterwards we used to get in a circle and dance and sing 'ring-o-roses' to get the blood moving in our arms.

Medical supplies were very hard to come by. People with

diabetes suffered particularly badly, as they soon ran out of the insulin they needed to stay well. Though the Red Cross had sent parcels which included medicine and food, contrary to the Geneva Convention, the Japanese mostly kept them for themselves. Once, cruelly, some children from the camp were made to pose with the parcels, as 'proof' they had been delivered, before they were confiscated again. After the war, the Allies would find warehouses piled full of Red Cross provisions. The only thing my family ever saw from those parcels was a tin of talcum powder, which was given to Mum.

Several of the women were pregnant when they first arrived at the camp. Our Katong friend Muriel Shorthouse was among the first to have her baby, whom she called Mervyn. I remember the afternoon he was born. I desperately wanted to see what was going on but Muriel's mother, Mrs McIntyre, shooed me away.

Altogether, 30 babies would be born to women interned at Changi jail. Most were delivered in the camp but some of the expectant mothers were allowed to go to the nearby Kandang Kerbau Hospital to give birth. When Daphne Davidson had her baby Jenny, the Japanese guards accompanying her took a photograph, supplying Mrs Davidson with a feeding bottle for the purposes of the picture. The Japanese obviously thought the photo would make good propaganda. Back at the camp, however, baby's bottles were in short supply.

Dental care was all but non-existent. Tooth brushes became as valuable as gold. Bandages were used and washed and used again. We were all covered in boils due to malnutrition but the only thing Dr Smallwood could do to treat them was heat the blade of a knife over a flame and drop it on the boil to cauterise it. We'd resorted to medieval standards of healthcare that matched our medieval standards of hygiene.

Everyone had sores and nits and everything else. How we hated the nits. There were always so many of them. I could feel them crawling down my neck constantly, driving me crazy. I would scrape them off by the handful. There were a couple of people in the camp who had brought nit combs in but they would never lend them to the rest of us.

Finger and toenails went unclipped. Mum had a couple of razor blades which she used to try to keep our nails short but they had to be kept hidden from the guards and the other internees. Likewise our soap, which we needed to wash ourselves and our clothes, had to be carefully guarded. When we showered, we would drop our knickers and knead them beneath our feet so that they were rinsed with the soapy run-off from our bodies.

At least while we were at Changi we occasionally got to bathe in the sea. The first Japanese commandant would task two or three of his guards with taking us children down to Changi beach in the evening in the hope that swimming in salt water would clean our skin and ease our sores. While we were there we'd look for cuttlefish bones that we could use as makeshift toothbrushes. Many children try to avoid cleaning their teeth but we were desperate to clean ours.

Down on the shore, we'd gather stones for playing 'five

stones' and on the way back to the camp, the guards would take us through rubber plantations, where we would stop to pick rubber nuts and leaves. We would fight over the passion fruit flowers and the little 'monkey cups' that filled with rain. Those monkey cups were actually carnivorous pitcher plants, which attracted flies and ants to their sticky deaths with their sweet nectar. When the passion fruit were ripe, we would work out where they were on the way down to the beach, then, on the way back to camp, when we got to the point where the fruit was growing, one of us would deliberately make a fuss and create a diversion so that the guards didn't see the other children swipe the valuable bounty that they would have otherwise taken for themselves.

The guards who took us to the beach were quite young and, I think, a little frightened of being in charge of so many child prisoners. They were relatively tolerant and usually let us take the time to mess around and act like the children we were. But they also took photographs of some of the children as they played to convince the outside world that we were all being well-treated. My brother Peter was told to pose for a photograph in which a guard offered him a jam sandwich.

'It was strawberry jam,' Peter told us.

'How did you know that?' the rest of us asked. Of course, he hadn't been allowed to eat it.

Once, on May 9th 1942, to mark a Japanese festival, the commandant permitted all the women in the camp to go to the beach for a celebratory bathe. It wasn't quite the privilege it seemed, as the trip had to be taken in the hottest part of the day.

All the same, the women made the most of it, shuffling down to the sand in their makeshift beach-wear and sun hats fashioned from scraps. They called it the 'Changi Stroll'.

28

GHOST STORIES

At certain times of the year, it was stiflingly hot around the clock so at night, instead of sleeping inside, we would lay down on the concrete paths outside E-block in a vain attempt to stay cool. We were always careful to ensure, when choosing our spots, that we weren't settling down on top of a colony of red ants who might eat us alive as we slept!

I loved to lay out there in the dark and learn all about the stars. It was comforting to look up at the heavens and see them looking back at us the same as always, no matter what was going on down below. I remember being delighted to see half the Southern Cross one night.

Another time we were very lucky to be lying in the right place at the right time to see the whole of the Southern Cross as it rose above the prison walls. It was wonderful to spot it. It felt like a blessing of sorts.

But it was on an evening like this that I had a very strange and unpleasant experience. I was in the E-block garden when I turned and saw what I first thought was a man, standing by the wall. However, it was not a Japanese guard or an emaciated man from the men's camp, but a being who appeared to be made entirely of sticks. It was a 'Hantu Galah' or 'pole ghost'.

I had heard stories of the Hantu Galah. In Johor Bahru, the children we played with often tried to scare us with tales of ghosts from Malay folklore, such as the Hantu Daguk, who appeared as mist, or the Hantu Pochong, a graveyard ghost who shuffled along swathed in a bundle of white rags in which he trapped unwitting humans. There were evil spirits galore but there were also playful ones, like the Hantu Batu, who liked to throw stones, and the Hantu Beruk, a demon monkey who could inhabit human beings and make them dance.

The Hantu Galah wasn't the worst of the spirits I'd been told about but it was especially uncanny. The creature moved like a giant insect through the forest and it was rumoured that if you walked between its legs, you would be transported to another dimension. I knew that the way to make the Hantu Galah disappear was to pick up a stick and snap it but that evening I could find none. Instead I froze and held my breath as the creature grew taller and taller in front of me until I could only see its legs. I didn't dare look up, since legend had it that if you looked up to see the face of a Hantu Galah, your head would be frozen in that position. Thankfully, after a moment or two, the creature on the wall at the camp simply seemed to disappear.

I didn't tell my friends what I had seen. I was afraid that they would laugh at me. The one person I felt I could have told was Dad but he was on the other side of the wall in the men's camp. Dad wouldn't have thought it strange, I was sure. Perhaps it was his Irish ancestry that meant he had always believed there was a world beyond the one we usually see.

When we lived in Johor Bahru, on certain days when Dad came back from work, he would tell Mum, 'She was there again today.'

'She' was a woman whom Dad said he often saw sitting on the tree stump at the end of our drive, as though she'd been waiting for him. A woman sitting on the stump wouldn't have been unusual, but the old woman was not one of the elderly ladies who lived in our village, stopping for a rest on her way back from the market. Dad said that this woman was young and dressed all in white, with long flowing hair. Apart from Dad, none of us had ever seen her.

I wonder now if the strange woman was a 'pontianak'. A pontianak was what the Malays called the spirit of a woman who died in childbirth. Malay folklore had it that the ghosts of such unlucky women were able to fly in the night. By day, they lived in the banana trees. They had razor-sharp teeth like a vampire's and they were often seen by the side of the road, hoping to find an unfortunate man to seduce.

Luckily, as soon as our father saw the pontianak and wished her 'good evening', she would disappear into thin air. She didn't seem to wish him or the rest of us any harm. It seemed to be enough for her that she was acknowledged. Neither did the Hantu Galah seem to want to hurt me. After that evening when he appeared on the prison wall in front of me, I never saw the pole ghost again.

29

THE CHANGI QUILTS

Changi might have been built as a prison and there's no doubt that we were prisoners, but to us children, Changi was just 'home'. It was the only place some of the younger children interned there had ever really known. I think it was far harder for the adults, knowing what they had lost and what might be coming next.

Many of the women in Changi had loved ones on the men's side of the camp – us included – and they were desperate for any news of them. A great deal of effort went into sending messages back and forth.

The fact that the food was prepared in the men's camp meant that there was at least one daily opportunity for the two halves of the camp to meet and exchange messages. The camp leaders on each side arranged rotas that meant that husbands and wives would be put on food duty at the same time, so that they might share just a couple of words or even touch each other's hands when the guards weren't looking. The women on food duty always made an effort to look their best when they saw their husbands through the barbed wire, dressing as carefully as they might have done to go to a dinner party or to the theatre in the days before the occupation.

We found other weak spots in the barriers between the camps. Near the showers, there was a gulley, covered with a wide steel grille. You could send something into the men's camp and vice versa using that gulley. Some of the more daring women would meet their menfolk there to talk through the grille. A few of them even managed to slip through the gulley and hold their husbands for a few precious minutes.

One day, the guards told us we would be allowed to receive presents from the men's camp. Dad sent Mum a coconut. It seemed like an incredible luxury and we looked forward to drinking the sweet coconut water.

Though we were desperate for something good to eat, Dad had realised this coconut might represent his only chance to get a message to us for a while. He had cleverly taken out one of the coconut's three 'eyes' so that he could poke a piece of paper inside. On the paper he'd written a few words in indelible pencil. Once the message was safely inside, Dad had resealed the hole to make it look as though the coconut was intact. We were thrilled when we cracked open the shell to eat the sweet white flesh and had the added bonus of seeing that tiny letter in Dad's familiar handwriting, telling us that he was well.

Despite the ingenuity of our games and the adults' contin-ued efforts to make sure we kept up with our school work, life in Changi could still be quite boring. We needed more to keep us occupied.

Among the women interned at the jail was Mrs Elizabeth Ennis, a nurse in the Indian army, newly married to a British pathologist, Captain Jack Ennis, who was being held on the other side of the camp. Before the occupation, Mrs Ennis had been a girl guide leader. Now she decided that what the camp needed was its very own guide group. I eagerly joined up. Our pack comprised 20 girls between the ages of eight and 16, supervised by Mrs Ennis and a couple of volunteers. We met weekly in the Carpenter's Shop. Such meetings brought another much-needed touch of normality to our lives.

Of course, we didn't have our official girl guide uniforms in camp, but we did cobble together a uniform of sorts – wearing white (in so far as our clothes had remained white) dresses when we met. We started our meetings with the usual girl guide salutes and promises. Then Mrs Ennis set us challenges, along the lines of those found in the guides' handbook. It was Mrs Ennis who taught us how to identify the stars upon which we gazed on clear nights.

We chose flowers as the emblems for our patrols. I picked edelweiss, the tiny white mountain daisy, and made badges featuring those flowers, using whatever materials we could lay our hands on. Rags became precious in camp. If a dress wore out, you didn't throw it away, but pulled it apart for threads and patches. Mum's decision to bring her sewing kit with her – a little raffia packet with needles, crochet hooks and a few cotton threads – proved to have been very wise indeed. That sewing kit suddenly became priceless.

We were all very fond of Mrs Ennis and wanted to give her some sort of present to show how much she was appreciated. Someone had the idea of making a quilt. It turned out to be the ideal project. A quilt could be made from the tiniest scraps of material and each of us could work on our own part in secret – keeping it from both Mrs Ennis and the Japanese guards – until we were ready to assemble the final piece. The plan was agreed. We would make the quilt in a traditional pattern known as 'grandmother's garden' and embroider our names in the centre of the flower motifs we stitched.

We started out thinking that we would make the quilt for Mrs Ennis's birthday, but soon realised that we did not know how long it would take. Fabric for the quilt was not easy to come by. We'd beg, steal or borrow whatever we could. Dresses rotted in the relentless sun, but the inside of a sleeve might survive, providing us with enough fabric to make a few squares. A Japanese woman who had been brought into the camp because her husband was English, gave us a strip of satin from the black trousers she always wore. The back of the quilt had to be made from calico flour bags. We used Mum's buttonhole scissors to cut out the pieces. Our secret sewing group met once a week, in a little hut with two small windows that let in just enough light to sew by.

Of course I asked to borrow one of Mum's needles to sew with. She gave me one with strict instructions that I had to look after it and return it to the sewing kit the very moment I had finished with it for the day. One day, I borrowed the needles, joined my friends and sewed for a little while as usual, but when I got back to the space on the floor where my family slept and kept our things, Mum was not there to take custody of the needle again. My sister Mary was so

I gave the precious needle to her, asking her to make sure Mum received it. Almost as soon as I had handed it over, Mary lost the needle but blamed me. I have rarely been in so much trouble with our mother as I was that day.

The sewing of the quilt was fraught with danger. We knew that if the Japanese caught us, we would be in big trouble but the risk felt worth it. Perhaps it even made the whole thing more fun. If we heard the guards coming, we would shove the piece of quilt we were working on down our knickers. I was lucky enough to have a yellow romper suit, made of 'trebalco' – a type of stiff cotton that was popular in Singapore – with elastic around the legs, which provided the ideal place to stash contraband. The elastic would keep my sewing in place when I had to stand and bow. But hiding our sewing was still a tricky enterprise. There wasn't usually time to take the needles out.

Keeping things hidden from the Japanese, who would search our belongings whenever they felt like it, was an ongoing challenge. But despite the obstacles we faced, the quilt was finished and we presented it to Mrs Ennis with pride.

Years later, she told a journalist from *The Telegraph* how proud she was that, 'Out of the grimness and misery of internment something so beautiful could be made by the guides who had lost all their possessions – but still had courage.'

Ours was not the only quilt to be made at Changi.

Mrs Mulvany, whose gift of a blue ribbon sash had made my first birthday as an internee so special, was inspired by the girl guides' ingenuity.

Having seen how we'd embroidered our names on the quilt we made for Mrs Ennis, Mrs Mulvany cleverly saw how the simple act of sewing might be turned to subterfuge.

Mrs Mulvany played a long game. Having gathered together a group of women in her own secret sewing bee, she first suggested that they make a very uncontroversial quilt, dotted with Japanese symbols. When the quilt was finished, Mrs Mulvany presented it to the guards, telling them that it was a gift to honour the Japanese dead.

Though there were very few women in the camp who felt like doing anything kind for the Japanese, Mrs Mulvany knew that a little bit of flattery would go a long way. The perfectly innocuous quilt lulled the Japanese into a false sense of security. What could be the harm of letting the women make further quilts, to be presented to the internees in the men's camp?

With an agreement in place that the quilts could be handed over by Red Cross representatives, the sewing bee went back to their sewing in earnest. This time, their embroidery had purpose. Mrs Ennis was among the women who made a patch for the next quilt, stitching it with a message for her husband Jack, whom she had not seen in 15 months. She embroidered a picture of an ocean liner, with the title 'Homeward Bound' and her name underneath.

Years later Mr and Mrs Ennis's daughter told *The Telegraph*, 'This message of hope and consolation, kept Jack going for the remainder of internment.'

Other messages were less cheerful. One woman embroidered a picture of someone in a cell, with the words, 'How long, dear Lord, how long?' But the men were uplifted to see the names of the women stitched into the fabric flowers, letting them know that their loved ones were still alive and keeping their spirits up and were determined that one day they would be together again.

30

MRS MULVANY

Ethel Mulvany was one of the most interesting women we met in Changi. Born and raised on Manitoulin Island, Canada, 20-year-old Ethel was on a tour of the Far East when she was taken ill on board a ship from Japan to Singapore en route to Thailand. The young doctor who cared for her was one Denis Mulvany, an Englishman. Having helped Ethel through her sickness, he soon fell in love with the unusually independent young woman. They spent the rest of the voyage getting to know one another and when they arrived in Singapore, Denis proposed marriage and Ethel abandoned her plan to 'visit the King of Siam'.

The Mulvanys spent the early years of their marriage in India, but in 1939 Denis was transferred to Singapore. Making the most of being near the sea, the Mulvanys built a boat and bought a small island, where they entertained their friends. They made a beautiful life in the city, but, like the rest of us, they found that beautiful life was not to last long. In February 1942, Mrs Mulvany was among the women who were marched from the Padang to Katong and thence to Changi.

I remember Mrs Mulvany as being larger than life. She

had an animated face with big features and a loud voice, which may have been because she was slightly deaf. Some of the adults seemed to find her style grating but I thought she was wonderful.

Mrs Mulvany was determined not to let prison life get the better of her. Before the occupation, she had volunteered for the Red Cross and she continued to bring that same sense of service to everything she did. From the elaborate 'tea parties' she threw to the 'silence hut' which she designed and had built, so that the adults might have a place where they could be free from the racket inside the prison buildings, Mrs Mulvany devoted herself to improving camp conditions for everyone.

In the early days at Changi, Mrs Mulvany persuaded the then camp commandant, Lieutenant Okasaki Tetsuji, to allow her to make trips to the local market, where, supervised by Japanese guards, she would scrounge or buy food for the rest of us, using money raised by trading what few valuable items we had left. Women would give her pieces of jewellery, including in some cases their wedding rings, to trade for such necessary items as a bar of soap or a jar of marmite. Conducting the trades in secret, she would bring money back into the camp in her shoes.

Mrs Mulvany always made sure to make the most of her time outside the camp to benefit those of us who didn't have such privileges. Each time she made a trip, she would take a different woman with her. She also had certain contacts in the outside world who did their best to assist her. Though some local people had jeered as we made the walk from Changi to Katong, there were others who went to extraordinary lengths to help us, at great risk to their own lives and those of their family members. The Japanese would not think twice about killing an entire family to make an example of them.

One of the locals who did his best to help Mrs Mulvany was a wealthy Chinese merchant called Seong. This kind man, who had known Mrs Mulvany before the war, would make it his business to run into her whenever she was in the market. On one occasion, in order to talk to Mrs Mulvany without drawing the suspicion of the Japanese guards accompanying her, Seong disguised himself as a beggar, and approached Mrs Mulvany as though he was going to ask her for money or food. Of course Mrs Mulvany recognised her contact but pretended not to, going so far as to pantomime the act of shooing him away. The brief encounter gave Seong just enough time to whisper 'buy five pumpkins from that stall'. Mrs Mulvany quickly agreed the purchase with the guards and brought the pumpkins back to E-block. When she cut them open, she discovered that the pumpkins had been hollowed out and stuffed with cash.

After that, pumpkins were often used for smuggling contraband into the camp. They were the perfect vegetable for such a purpose. It was easy to take the stalk out and make a hollow to hide a letter or medicine inside before putting the stalk back in.

Mrs Mulvany's daring made life better for all of us. She had a tiny radio, on which she secretly listened to reports from the outside world, passing on any good news to the rest of us. She was also good at raising our spirits by engaging us in conversations about the good things we remembered about our lives before the war. She would gather some of the women together over a tea table set with imaginary linen and porcelain to describe their favourite meals in minute detail. My sister Mary was among those who joined Mrs Mulvany to swap recipes from our Johor Bahru days.

Mrs Mulvany had a powerful personality and was not easily cowed. While the rest of us kept our heads down, she never hesitated to stand up to the guards if she felt she had to. She was fearless. I remember once, when we were all settling down for the night, Mrs Mulvany got into an argument with a guard who was walking through the hall. I don't know what the argument was about but Mrs Mulvany stood her ground and continued to do so until the guard unsheathed the sword he had been wearing on his belt and brandished it at her, threatening to slice off her head if she didn't shut up. As the blade flashed in front of her face, Mrs Mulvany backed away, but we all knew that by forcing the guard to lose control, she had really won the fight. In another incident, she attacked a Japanese general and had to be chained to the top of a table to restrain her.

Mrs Mulvany came with us from Changi to Sime Road when we moved, where she continued to be a thorn in the side for the Japanese.

From time to time, she was still allowed to go to the market on behalf of the rest of us. I remember Eileen and I were laying out on the hillside at Sime Road one day when we saw Mrs Mulvany and her escort come back from a shopping trip. They were stopped just inside the gate for a search. The Japanese guards were very strict about checking the car to make sure that Mrs Mulvany had only brought back what had already been agreed with their superiors. Eileen and I watched as Mrs Mulvany was made to stand to the side while the guard on duty at the gate was looking the vehicle over. He found nothing untoward. But after the guard had walked off, we saw Mrs Mulvany lift the cushion of the car's passenger seat out and retrieve dozens of fresh eggs that she had hidden in the seat's springs.

Mrs Mulvany kept in touch with Seong, the merchant who had disguised himself as a beggar. When she was no longer allowed to go to the market, Seong's grandson used to come to the camp each night to pass on contraband and information. He and Mrs Mulvany would lay down on the ground on either side of the fence and talk to each other through the gaps. Their conversations were not only important as a means of exchanging information; through their secret chats Mrs Mulvany and Seong's grandson forged a valuable friendship.

One day, the young man told Mrs Mulvany that he wouldn't be coming to see her anymore. He was going to be executed the following morning. He said that one of his friends had taken his place in line so that he could come to say 'goodbye'. This probably seems odd to a western reader. Who would take someone's place in a line to be executed? But such a gesture would not have seemed strange to the Singaporean

Chinese, who believed that friendship was a sacred thing and that we owe our friends as much support and honour as we owe our families. Having bid Mrs Mulvany goodbye, Seong's grandson returned to his fate. He was just 18 years old when he was killed.

Prior to the war, Mrs Mulvany had been diagnosed with bipolar disorder – manic depression as it was known back then. The death of Seong's grandson led Mrs Mulvany to have a full-blown breakdown.

Then came the awful day when one of the other women in the camp told the Japanese guards about Mrs Mulvany's radio in exchange for extra rations. She was taken away and tortured and then put into solitary confinement. She continued to torment the Japanese from her cell, singing at the top of her voice. When one of the guards tried to shut her up by threatening her with his bayonet, she grabbed him round the neck and almost choked him to death. She received a certain strange respect from the Japanese after that.

Mrs Mulvany made it to the end of the war but life was not especially kind to her in the aftermath. Upon leaving Sime Road, she spent a brief period in India, recovering her strength before, together with her husband Denis, she sailed to England, where she was hospitalised at the Bethlem Royal Hospital (the notorious 'Bedlam') and treated with electroshock therapy. When she was released from hospital, Denis sent Mrs Mulvany back to Canada alone, to live with an aunt and uncle. Denis subsequently asked her for a divorce.

Devastated by the end of her marriage and without any money of her own, Mrs Mulvany had to rely on the kindness of her relatives in Toronto. There followed a couple of difficult years. Badly affected by her time in Changi and Sime Road, Mrs Mulvany became a compulsive eater and hoarder. She was consumed by her hatred of the Japanese. However, at the end of those two years, Mrs Mulvany seemed to rediscover something of her old self.

Remembering those nights in Changi, when the women shared memories of their favourite meals, Mrs Mulvany compiled a cookbook of all the recipes she could remember. She took her notes to a local printer and, using the charm that had got her out of all sorts of scrapes in camp, persuaded him to print a number of copies, promising that she would pay him once the books had been sold. In the end, Mrs Mulvany sold 3000 copies of her POW recipe book, raising $18,000 (the equivalent of $200,000 in today's money), which she used to send oranges, tea and cigarettes to ex-POWs still languishing in hospitals in England. The book contained a cake recipe written by my sister.

Later, Mrs Mulvany created an initiative called the 'Treasure Van', which toured Canada and the United States, selling craft items made in India and the Far East to raise funds for the artisans' communities. Despite, or perhaps because of her experiences in Singapore, Mrs Mulvany always remained keen to foster international understanding. She believed that knowing something of another culture's traditions might break down the barriers that so often led to war.

In the 1960s, Mrs Mulvany gave a series of interviews to a journalist who published a piece about her in a magazine called Maclean's. Mrs Mulvany used the $500 dollars she was paid for the article to help a young friend – a Japanese student called Isami Endo, be reunited with his fiancée Shigeko, who was still in Japan. What's most surprising about this gesture is that Shigeko knew nothing of their kind benefactor's time in the camps until many years later.

Mrs Mulvany died in Canada in1992, at the age of 87. I will never forget her kindness or the blue ribbon sash that she gave to me on my 10th birthday.

31

BALSAM AND BLUE STOCKING

Mrs Mulvany's encounter with the guard who brandished his sword was very upsetting to see. Fortunately, not all of the guards had a sword, but they always carried some sort of weapon – usually a stick or a truncheon. How we hated the sight of those things, knowing the pain they could inflict only too well. We quickly learned how to read our captors' body language and if we ever saw a guard with his hand on his truncheon, we made sure to give him a very wide berth.

We were not allowed to mix with the guards and certainly could not make friends with them. They expected nothing but respect from us prisoners. We had to bow to them each morning. We had to bow again whenever we encountered them during the course of the day. We had to bow in the evening too. If you didn't bow correctly, which meant bending straight from the hips at a 90-degree angle, you would be whipped with a cane. Whippings were commonplace. Most of the guards were indifferent to our suffering. They saw us as something less than human.

The most senior of the guards at Changi was called Tommy

Right: Eileen, Stella and their mother visiting us in Tampoi. I used to look upon Eileen and Stella as film stars, they always looked so lovely

Left: I was the second of my parents' four children. My big sister Mary was born in 1929. I followed in 1932. We had two younger brothers, Peter and George

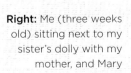

Right: Me (three weeks old) sitting next to my sister's dolly with my mother, and Mary

Top: Me, my siblings and our neighbour with the python we briefly kept as a pet

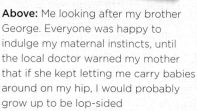

Above: Me looking after my brother George. Everyone was happy to indulge my maternal instincts, until the local doctor warned my mother that if she kept letting me carry babies around on my hip, I would probably grow up to be lop-sided

Left: Keyno and me. I'm wearing a baju kurung – traditional Malaysian dress

Above: Moving home from Tampoi to Johor Bahru

Left: Leaving Changi Beach after the Christmas holidays (1941). I'm holding my Betsy Wetsy doll

Above: Mary and me with our pet guinea pigs in Singapore

Top left: I *(right)* hated being dressed up for Christmas

Right: Taken in the garden at Johor Bahru (*from left to right*: George, our amah, Peter, Mary, Pacheum and me)

Below: Going to a party. I still remember my mother's mauve dress and the deep violet flowers on her hat

Top right: Christmas with the three Russian sisters we met in Singapore, including my namesake Olga

Right: At the Red Cross Station in Columbo, where we were supplied with clothes and toys for our journey to the UK in October 1945

Left: Mum, me and my brothers back in Singapore after the war

Right: A photo of Mary in England (c. 1948) where she trained to be a nurse after the war. Mary had been encouraged to pursue a medical career by Tommy Ryan, the boy from camp who'd sent me that beautiful birthday card

With all my love Mary

Top left: One day I found just enough paper to make a paper doll and a wardrobe full of clothes for her

Top right: April with her pet dogs

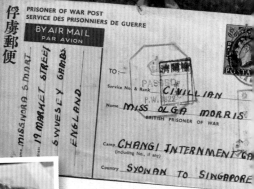

Above: A rare card sent from Changi to a cousin I'd never met

Left: The little china cat found by Mr Robertson at Hiroshima. She had a thin layer of ash on her bottom, but released from the glass, she was otherwise perfect

Right: Marrying Jim was the happiest day of my life. It was a beautiful day. I wore a dress made for me by the Japanese tailor who had made clothes for Mum before the occupation

Below: My contribution to the 'Changi quilt' with my name embroidered in the centre

Above: The quilt that I helped to make for Mrs Ennis, our girl guide leader, is now in the Imperial War Museum in London. I visited with my daughter Catriona, my granddaughter Emma and my great-granddaughter Bella, known as Bea

Top: Laying a wreath with my friend Wilma Howe, who had also been at Sime Road camp. That year, 2017, marked the 75th anniversary of the fall of Singapor

Above: With my friend Eileen Harris, who was interned along with me at Chang and Sime Road

Naga. He was a horrible piece of work. He was a big man with a loud, booming voice and he would find any excuse to hit you. Not bowing correctly was just the start with Tommy. Then there was 'Artichoke Joe', so called because his ears were the shape of artichoke leaves.

There were two guards in particular that everybody hated. They were nicknamed 'Balsam' and 'Blue Stocking'. Blue Stocking was given his name for the blue feather he always wore tucked into the long socks which he wore with khaki shorts. I don't know how Balsam came to get his name but while he might have been named after the sweet-scented sap of a flower, Balsam was far from pleasant. He always carried a stick and was always in a terrible temper. He would walk around E-block thrashing the hell out of the grass, doubtless imagining that he was thrashing the hell out of us as he went.

There was however one guard we did come to appreciate. He was quite a young man, with a lovely round face, and he patrolled the fence between the men's and women's camps. The Japanese had this funny protocol where if one guard or sergeant had been ticked off and perhaps even smacked by his superior, he could pass the anger down to the corporal, who could pass it on to the private, who passed it on to us if we happened to get in the way. The anger would go all the way down. But if this particular young guard saw that an angry superior was coming our way, he'd feign a bad cough to let us know that someone was on the warpath and give us a chance to hide. So among all those guards who would give you the whip as soon as they saw you, there was at least one man who tried to protect us child internees in his own small way.

While that guard protected us from some of the physical pain, nothing could protect us child prisoners from the psychological effects of being in the camp. Our mothers did their best to shield us from the worst and tried to make sure that we continued to act like the well-brought up children they had always intended us to be, but when the adults weren't looking, things were different. As with any group of children, thrown together by circumstance – by living in the same street or going to the same school, for example – the children in the camp formed alliances and enmities. And the violence we had witnessed prior to and during our internment was sometimes played out in our games, particularly among the younger children.

There was one awful incident at Changi where a group of younger children became obsessed with finding out whether it was true that when someone is hanged, their feet kick uncontrollably as they die. They decided there was only one way to find out. They built a makeshift gallows and persuaded the smallest child in the gang to put his neck in the noose. Luckily, one of the adults stumbled upon the horrific scene before the poor boy was killed.

But how can you blame children for imitating what they've seen and heard about from the adults in their lives? The spectacle of casual cruelty and death had become far too familiar to us all.

32

THE RINGS

One of the things we had to do in Changi was work the land around the building. The children were each given a patch of earth to cultivate along the rain gulley beside the prison wall. There we grew aubergines, chilis and kang kung, though you can be sure we never saw the results of our labour on our dinner plates. The moment anything ripened, we had to inform the Japanese guards, who would pick the harvest and keep it all for themselves. The next day, we would be allowed back to dig over the land and start the process all over again. We weren't even given tools for our labours. I fashioned myself a spade out of a piece of tree bark. It wasn't easy to dig a garden with such a flimsy implement. All the same, I took pride in my work.

After my first harvest at Changi had been collected by the guards, I set about preparing the earth for the next crop. Having grown up on a farm, Mum knew how to get the best of the land and advised me to be sure that I turned the soil over properly before I added any new plants. That meant digging deep. As I was doing exactly that, I came across a piece of waxed green material, which I recognised as being the sort of material engineers used to protect plans from hungry ants. Dad had lots of it in the house in Johor Bahru. What was that doing there, I wondered. I tugged the scrap out of the ground and put it to one side.

Moments later, a glint of metal caught my eye and I dug up something much more interesting than that scrap of green material. It was a ring. A ladies' ring set with a jewel. I couldn't believe it. Without raising the alarm, I quietly slipped the ring on my finger and continued to dig in the same spot. Every other spadeful of earth revealed more treasure and before I knew it, I had found a ring for every finger. I shoved them all on and hurried back into E-block with my hands thrust deep in my pockets, praying that no-one would stop me before I could get back to our room.

Mum was as astonished as I had been to see the bounty that I'd found. We brushed the dirt off and examined my treasure trove closely. They were beautiful rings. Obviously valuable. How had they come to be in my vegetable patch? Someone must have hidden them there, wrapped in that green material. But who? And when? I didn't think they had been put there recently. Those rings had been deep in the earth and the grass had grown over them. I was sure that they must have already been there when I planted my first crop.

Mum came outside to see where I had found the rings and told me that we needed to keep quiet. Apart from Mum and I, the only person who knew about the rings was April, who was sharing our room. Mum asked her to look after three of four of them, so that they weren't all in the same place. April agreed. She wrapped her share of the rings in a hand-kerchief and pinned them to her knickers for safe-keeping.

We knew we could trust April. In the short time we'd been sharing a room, she had proven herself to be a good friend to our family. We were sure the rings were safe with her. But unfortunately, the rings were too heavy for the worn-out fabric of April's hankie and later that day, as she was walking down the corridor, a couple of them dropped to the floor with a clatter.

In a flash, a Chinese lady from the next room claimed them, saying they were hers. When April said they were mine, the Chinese lady accused me of having stolen them. She said that I must have gone into her room while she was working outside and found the rings in their hiding place beneath her mattress. It was a ridiculous accusation. The Chinese women had their beds right up against the far wall and covered with blankets. No casual thief would have tried to get anything from under there.

Mum and April both knew that the Chinese woman was lying. Those rings hadn't been found in any room. Her story didn't fit the facts at all. But another Chinese internee backed the first woman up and the news that I had stolen the rings soon spread around the prison.

The row drew a crowd. Mum stood up for me and asked Dr Smallwood to adjudicate, sure that Dr Smallwood would believe my version of events. Mum assured the doctor that I was not a liar. I hadn't been raised that way. Mum would know at once if I had done something wrong. And there was no way the rings came from the Chinese women's room. They were still covered in dirt when Mum first saw them. We took Dr Smallwood to see my vegetable patch. I showed her the rotten green material that had alerted me to the rings' presence. I thought that when she saw the hole I'd dug, and how deep it was, she would understand at once that I was telling the truth, but to my horror Dr Smallwood would not take a side. She would not defend me.

There was so much shouting and anguish about the whole affair that it wasn't long before the Japanese guards came to find out what was going on. They took over. I don't know what happened to the rings after that but I'm pretty sure that the Japanese wouldn't have let the Chinese women keep them. All of us lost.

It was bad enough to have been accused of stealing and to have lost the rings which might have been bartered for food, but worse was to come. My whole family was punished for my refusal to own up to a crime I had not committed.

Dr Smallwood and the other senior women in the camp called a meeting to work out what should be done. It was decided that my family would lose the room where we had been sleeping and move instead to a place by the door outside E-block in the corridor, by the steel doors, where we had to sleep directly on the concrete floor. Furthermore, Mum was to be given the role of 'gate wallah' – which meant opening the door to the Japanese soldiers, who made sure that she had to get up and down all night long to let them into the corridor. It wasn't just a matter of opening the big steel door then going back to bed. We all had to bow to the guards every time they came in and if we were too tired to bow low enough – we had to bow to that perfect 90 degree angle no matter how late at night – there would be trouble. We then had to stand and wait until the guards had finished their checks and were ready to leave. They would take their time and laugh about it. They knew they were ruining our chance of sleep.

After a long period in the corridor, we were moved into one of the cells on the first floor of E-block when some other poor soul was given the 'gate wallah' job. This was no real improvement. The cells were only eight feet wide by 12 feet long, but seven of us were crammed into each one. We were joined by Loulou Martin, a young Armenian woman who was very religious. There was nowhere near enough room for seven people to sleep in those tiny boxes, especially since in the middle of the floor was a concrete platform that served as a single bed. We had to take it in turns to stretch out on that unforgiving 'mattress' and at other times would have to try to sleep sitting, or just stand there in the dark. Each cell had a squatting toilet in one corner, which worked well enough until it blocked. You can't imagine how unpleasant that was.

The cells had only one small window, right at the top of the wall. We children used to climb on each other's shoulders to look out. The walls were rough brick and we realised on that very first night that the crevices hid bed bugs. We made a game of digging them out and squashing them. Those vile black bugs smelled disgusting.

It was horrible, first to be in the corridor and then in that cell. After the incident with the rings, we felt very much as though our family had been 'put aside' by the women in charge. The accusation of theft seemed impossible to shake off. Though she would never speak about it and I didn't ask, I know that the whole affair affected Mum dreadfully, while I burned with indignation at the thought of having been accused of a crime I had not committed. I could not believe that what had seemed like such a stroke of luck – finding such treasure in my vegetable patch – could have turned out so badly for all of us.

33

PROPAGANDA

For the women and girls at Changi, guarded exclusively by men, the threat of sexual violence was always present. After the Japanese took Hong Kong, some of their soldiers went on the rampage, raping and killing the unfortunate women they came across. Even nurses, who had stayed on in the Far East to help the dying, were submitted to the most terrible violence.

When the Japanese came to Singapore, their commanding officers made clear that such behaviour would not be tolerated, but how could we be reassured? Who knew what those men who beat us for the slightest infraction might be capable of doing if no-one else was around to see?

They saw us as objects. While we were in the showers in the evening, they would take it in turns to sit in chairs that had been placed so they had a front row view of us washing ourselves. They did not even pretend that they were on some official duty. They would sit there with their hands down their shorts. They were quite blatant about it and there was nothing we could do. Though they professed to hate white women, the Japanese guards seemed to find our bodies endlessly fascinating. It was disgusting. There was glee in the way the Japanese guards humiliated and punished us for the crime of being European.

One day while we were at Changi, Mum, my brothers and I got back to our cell after breakfast and found that my sister Mary was missing. Mary was beautiful. Blonde and pretty. She was only 14 but looked older. When we couldn't find her, everyone was frantic with worry. While we searched all the cells, the Japanese woman who was stuck in the prison because she had been married to an English soldier, came to find us. The Japanese guards hated her for having married a white man and treated her especially harshly, but she would often intercede for us in their language. She told us that she had found out by eavesdropping that three guards had taken Mary out of the prison and into the woods. When she heard this news, Mum was beside herself.

It could only mean one thing. The soldiers must have taken Mary into the woods with the very worst intentions. But while Mum and I desperately tried to work out what on earth we could do, Mary suddenly walked back into E-block, completely unaware of the panic caused by her disappearance and looking totally unscathed by her adventure.

Had the Japanese woman heard wrongly? No. She had not. The Japanese soldiers had indeed taken Mary into the woods, but they hadn't tried to rape or otherwise abuse her. Instead, they'd made her sit on the stump of a tree and given her a book to read while they took photographs.

The pictures were for propaganda purposes. Presumably, they were going to be used to show the outside world how well the Japanese were treating their prisoners. 'Look how kind we are! We even let them climb trees and read novels!'

Mary laughed as she told us what had happened. 'They put the book in my lap upside down.'

The fact that Mary had not been sexually assaulted came as a huge relief. It didn't make us trust the Japanese soldiers any better though. From that day forward, it was decided that Mary should never be left alone again. Dr Smallwood arranged that Mary would be moved into the small room at the end of the block where April now slept. That way, Mary could be kept out of sight as much as possible. April was by then in her late thirties or forties. She knew all there was to know about men and could tell when the Japanese soldiers were circling. April assured us that under her watchful eye, Mary would come to no harm. The same was done for Ozzie's sister Olive, who had grown into a very beautiful young woman. The camp leaders made sure she was never on her own.

We were still very angry at the thought that Mary's image would be used to maintain a lie about the treatment of internees. The Japanese were very fond of propaganda. Among the people I met later on in the war was my friend Wilma Stubbs and her five siblings. Wilma's mother was Eurasian and her father was a British doctor. They had been picked up by the Japanese in Sumatra, then brought to Singapore where they were allowed to live at large in the city, so long as they always wore a red circle – reminiscent of the Star of David badges the Jewish people had been made to wear in Nazi-occupied Europe. The experiment lasted three months, then the Japanese brought the Stubbs family to Sime Road camp, which of course, the Japanese still called a 'civil internment centre', where we 'internees' were being held for our own 'protection'.

34

THE 'DOUBLE TENTH'

In September 1943, the Japanese military in Singapore was shocked by a series of acts of sabotage. Telephone lines were cut and warehouses were set on fire. Then, on September 28th, six Japanese oil tankers were blown up in Singapore Harbour. This spectacular attack was a huge blow to the Japanese sense of superiority. How had the saboteurs managed to creep into the harbour right under their noses?

The Kempeitai, the Japanese special police, immediately set about finding the culprits. Lieutenant Colonel Haruzo Sumida, who was leading the investigation, became convinced that the saboteurs must have been organised by internees in Changi, in collaboration with Singaporeans on the outside. Sumida immediately ordered a raid on the prison to find evidence for his hypothesis.

On October 10th – a day that would become known as the 'Double Tenth' – the Kempeitai raided our camp and the men's camp next door. They made us all stand outside E-block in the blazing heat while they searched every nook and cranny for the secret radio sets they were sure had been used to pass on Japanese military information. The search went on for an age. Without shade or water, many of the women and children standing outside that day fainted but we were forbidden from helping anyone who fell.

After many hours of hunting, during which time they turned our few belongings upside down, the Japanese found some wire in the women's camp. That was all. However not long afterwards a homemade wireless set was discovered in the men's camp.

Several male internees were immediately taken to the Kempeitai headquarters in the city's old YMCA building. A little later three women from our camp – Dorothy Nixon, Dr Cicely Williams and Freddy Bloom – were also taken in for questioning.

Freddy Bloom was well-known about the camp as one of Mrs Milne's volunteer teachers. My sister Mary adored her. As well as helping Mrs Milne set up her school, Freddy had started a secret camp newsletter, called Pow Wow. It was a valuable publication, raising the morale of every prisoner who got to read it.

Unfortunately for Freddy, her involvement with the newsletter was enough to make Lieutenant Colonel Haruzo Sumida suspect she was also involved in a spy ring feeding information to the guerrillas who had blown up the Japanese tankers. That was why she was hauled up before the secret police.

Dorothy Nixon was originally from Yorkshire and had worked as a Land Girl in WW1. She'd come to Malaya to join her husband, who was working on a rubber plantation. Later, she became Head Librarian at the Kuala Lumpur

Book Club, which provided a mail-order library service for expats in remote areas of the country. At the time of the Double Tenth, she had recently resigned her position as our women's commandant. During her six-month long tenure, she had frequently butted heads with the Japanese commandant.

I'm not sure why Dr Williams should have fallen under suspicion. Born in Jamaica, she'd studied medicine in Oxford during WW1, when the rules about female medical students were relaxed. She became a paediatrician and, since work for female doctors was still limited in the 1920s, joined the Colonial Service, which took her to Malaya. Before the war she had campaigned against the promotion of baby formula to the poor. She delivered most of the babies who were born in the camp.

When Freddy Bloom, Dorothy Nixon and Dr Williams were taken away, we children didn't really know what was going on. All we heard was the whisper that 'somebody else has gone out'. Shielded from the truth by the adults, we assumed the women must have been taken ill. The Japanese were very frightened of an epidemic breaking out amongst the prisoners lest it spread to the guards. The moment any one of the prisoners showed signs of something that might cause a problem – if they had a cough that suggested tuberculosis, for example – they were sent straight to the hospital.

We know now that the internees who were taken from Changi on the Double Tenth were subjected to the most horrific torture imaginable. One man had a pipe put down his throat and another up his backside. The pipes were attached to the taps and then the water was turned on. Several of the men tried to commit suicide.

The women did not fare any better. They were held in a small wooden cell with 15 men. During the day they were forced to sit cross-legged. A bright light that could not be turned off kept them awake at night. The only source of water was an open toilet.

Dorothy Nixon spent one month in the crowded cell before she was put into solitary confinement for a further five months. She was all but starved to death, given only condensed milk to eat.

Though they were not physically tortured, Freddy Bloom and Dr Williams were questioned many times and were forced to listen to the agonised screams of their male cellmates as they were subjected to unimaginable feats of cruelty. Later, they were forced to watch some of the men die.

Dr Williams lost a third of her body weight and contracted beriberi – a disease caused by vitamin B1 deficiency, which was why Marmite became so important to everyone in the camp as a valuable source of B vitamins. By the time Dr Williams was released back into Changi, her hair had gone completely grey.

Freddy was held by the Kempeitai for five months, during which time she also developed severe beriberi. She then went on to have two heart attacks, which were no doubt brought on by malnutrition. It was only after the second heart attack that the Kempeitai decided there was no point in continuing to question her.

As well as the women taken from Changi, the Japanese

had also taken in a Singaporean Chinese woman called Elizabeth Choy, whose husband Choy Khun Heng, was believed to have smuggled money and radio equipment into the men's camp. Elizabeth Choy was horribly humiliated. At one point, she was stripped to the waist and tied down before the Japanese subjected her to a series of electric shocks. Her husband was forced to watch her being tortured and vice versa. Elizabeth Choy was held prisoner and tortured for 200 days.

In total, of the 57 people taken in for questioning on the Double Tenth, 15 died. What was especially sad was that none of them had actually known anything about the commando raids and the sinking of the Japanese ships. Those confessions which had been dragged from them with such brutality were meaningless.

In fact, the attack on Singapore Harbour had been carried out by British and Australian commandos from 'Z' Special Unit, under the leadership of Lieutenant Colonel Ivan Lyon. The commandos had rowed into the harbour under cover of darkness on folding canoes and attached limpet mines to the Japanese ships. They made their escape on an old Japanese fishing boat called The Krait. The mission, called Operation Jaywick, had not involved any of the men and women the Japanese had questioned and tortured.

For many years after the horror of the Double Tenth, local people claimed that if you walked by the old YMCA building between two and four o'clock in the morning, you could hear the sound of people crying out in fear and agony.

Many wouldn't walk by the building at all – by night or by day – so sad and painful were the memories of everything that had happened there.

All we knew at the time was that the regime at Changi had changed for good. We heard that the Japanese commandant with the American wife and two daughters was shot for having been too kind to us. All our privileges were revoked. There were no more concerts. No more lessons. No more visits to the beach to wash away the lice. No more than four people were allowed to meet at any time and that included children. Our guide troop could not meet any more. At any time of the day or night, our quarters might be searched. Our food rations were cut down to next to nothing.

The Japanese were determined to show us just how viciously they could respond to any military humiliation. Our life was reduced to waiting for the next meal, wondering if and when the war would ever end.

Sime Road

"We were ravaged night and day by malaria-carrying mosquitoes. We had boils under our arms all the time. Our hair was full of nits and we couldn't cut our finger or toenails because we weren't allowed to have scissors."

PART FOUR

MAY 1944 – SEPTEMBER 1945

35

ON THE MOVE AGAIN

We had been in Changi for just over two years, when in May 1944 it was announced that we were to be moved elsewhere. The Japanese had decided that they wanted to use the jail to house Allied soldiers, injured or taken ill during their work on the building of the notorious Thailand-Burma railway – known as the 'Death Railway'. Those men had been held at Sime Road, the site of the former combined operational headquarters of the British Army and Royal Air Force, but as the Allies began the push back in the Far East, the Japanese were concerned that Sime Road would not be secure enough in the event of a prisoner uprising. Changi Jail was far safer. It was to be a straight swap. The injured soldiers would be moved into our camp and we civilians would move into theirs.

At least we would not have to walk to our new home. It was 13 miles from Changi to Sime Road and I'm not sure that many of us would have made it, hungry and malnourished as we were. Instead, we were loaded onto open trucks. It was easier than marching but it was a far from comfortable ride as we travelled slowly cross-country along tiny dirt roads that rattled our bones with every bump. Only the smaller children were able to sit down. The rest of us had to stand up and hang on tight.

Though we could have jumped, we all knew by now that it was not even worth thinking about trying to escape. In our weakened state, we wouldn't have got far. Instead, we stood still and gazed out, taking in the landscape as we drove by. For many of us, this was the first time we had seen the outside world in more than two years. The locals looked downtrodden and unhappy. They looked hungry too and seemed as cowed by the Japanese as we were. Two and a half years of war had broken everyone.

Conditions at Changi had not been luxurious but things were about to get much worse. With only injured men kept there, the Sime Road station had been allowed to fall into disrepair. Long grass grew everywhere. In places it was taller than we were. All the buildings looked shabby and uncared for, though the blue painted sign still hung from outside The Flying Dutchman, which had once been the office where the RAF men clocked in and out. The Flying Dutchman would become the headquarters for the women's side of the camp.

Upon arrival we were told to take our things into a large hut – Hut 16. The ramshackle shed had been built to house 34 airmen. Now there were 134 women and children to cram in. We found ourselves a corner and marked it out with our sleeping mats and the wicker basket that contained all that we had left in the world. Mary stuck close by April. They had been allocated their own small room at the opposite end of the hut to me, Mum and the boys.

You can't imagine how filthy the place was. Hut 16 had all but fallen down before we arrived. The roof, which was made of palm fronds laid over asbestos, leaked and the sides of the hut were more or less open to the elements. When it rained, there was nothing we could do but huddle together in the very middle, in a desperate attempt to stay dry. There were no lights, which meant we wouldn't be able to do anything like read or sew after sunset. The only time we could really see in the hut at night time was if there was a full moon, which shone through the gaps in the ceiling. We would fix the hut up as best we could but it was a losing battle from the start. The chickens we'd kept in Johor Bahru had better living conditions.

The washing facilities were far worse. At Changi, there was always water and there were even some flush toilets. There were no such luxuries here. The toilets at Sime Road were simply pits in the ground, covered with tea chests with holes in them that served as makeshift seats. They were disgusting. There was no privacy as the commandant would not allow them to be covered by a hut. They stank to high heaven and were crawling with maggots. When we first arrived, we found that a toad had made its home in one of the pits. It kept us awake, squawking loudly all night long.

And every day more people arrived. We didn't know where we were supposed to put them. We later heard that on the men's side of the camp, 604 Jewish men were crammed into a hut the same size as ours.

There was just one lovely building left at Sime Road. Right at the top of the camp was a big house, built for the British military commanders who had once led the base.

The Japanese officers took that for their quarters, of course. Around it they had prisoners plant them a beautiful garden, where they could find respite from the horror of their duties (and the horrors they inflicted on us). For us, at Sime Road, there was just an eight foot wide strip of sandy soil, where nothing seemed to grow.

We had a new home and a new regime. After the Double Tenth, discipline in the camps had been tightened. At Changi, we had been relatively free to mingle but there was none of that any more. Suddenly, the Japanese were much more strict about making sure they knew our whereabouts at all times.

At Sime Road, 'tenko' – the Japanese word for roll call – became more important than ever. Every morning and every evening, each and every one of us had to stand outside our hut to be counted by the guards. We lined up in the exact same spot every time. Standing there, perfectly still and silent, we would have to hope that the officers would finish their inspections before someone fainted. They would walk around the back of us and if we didn't bow long enough or deeply enough, they would hit us with a stick. Our hearts all sank when we first got to Sime Road and realised that those horrible guards Balsam and Blue Stocking had been transferred to the new camp with us.

When tenko was over, a tub of food was brought up to us for breakfast and we'd eat our measly share. We were all so hungry that the job of washing the tubs (and perhaps stealing a few extra grains) became a sort of privilege. A rota had to be drawn up to make sure that we all got our turn. It was terrible but we got used to it. What else could we do?

There was no privacy and no dignity. At night, the guards would come into the huts and shine torches on us in our night-clothes. The excuse was that they had to check we were wearing our identification badges, which were supposed to be worn even while we slept. But they only ever looked at the young women and girls.

36

THE LITTLE MATCH GIRL

Just like Changi, at Sime Road prisoners were expected to grow food for the Japanese guards. We grew more kang kung, which we were occasionally permitted to add to our food for much needed vitamins. There was also a tapioca field where we would work in the blazing sun, wearing whatever we could find to protect our heads. Some of the women made fabulous creations from old rice sacks and cardboard.

In addition to tending the gardens and the tapioca, we were expected to work elsewhere on the camp. Japan's Prime Minister Hideki Tojo had ordered that internees be used as slave labour and that's exactly what happened. Everyone was put to work, from the most elderly adults right down to the smallest children. Now 12 years old, I was first given a job knitting socks for the Japanese soldiers. I'd always liked knitting, but not now. The stringy yarn was rough and it was hard on your hands. The strands came apart, making it difficult to use. In addition to making the socks, I had to finish off the buttonholes in Japanese soldiers' caps.

Meanwhile my sister Mary worked as a seamstress, making

five Japanese army shirts a day on a sewing machine that had been brought into the camp for this purpose. The shirts were pre-cut so that the women putting them together had no access to scissors. Mary and her co-workers in the shirt factory sewed from dawn until dusk. It was difficult work, especially as the light fell. It was almost impossible to see in that hut if it was raining outside.

There were always so many shirts to sew and caps to finish and there was no question of not getting them done. Each day, our captors would check on our productivity. If we weren't up to speed, if not enough socks had been made or buttonholes finished, well, then we were punished. The main punishment the Japanese employed was cutting our already meagre rations but there were other, crueller, punishments too. One of the worst was being made to kneel on stony ground for hours at a time. We were punished for anything and everything and there's no doubt that some of the guards took pleasure in it. The regime was very frightening for children like us who had grown up thinking that 'punishment' was not being allowed to read the comics because you'd been cheeky to your parents.

I did my knitting and finishing off the buttonholes alone, but later I was set to work in the match factory that had been built on the site. My job was to dip matches into hot wax to protect them from the humidity. I sat at a bench on the back row alongside my friends Eileen and Ozzie. We each had a little burner on which we'd have our wax pots. We'd dip the matches one by one, then, when they were dry, we'd pack them into boxes. We didn't have any special clothing to protect us from wax spills and the like. We weren't that valuable. I didn't even have a pair of shoes, having long since grown out of the ones I'd had at Changi.

We spent many hours a day in the match factory, in return for only a little extra rice at mealtimes. There was no longer any time for lessons or for putting on concerts and plays. We were no longer officially allowed to associate with our fellow internees or gather in groups unless it was for a particular job. At the end of each working day we would simply head back to Hut 16, hoping that no-one would have stolen our place on the floor while we were away. You kept to your spot all the time. There was nowhere to go.

That said, there were a few memorable occasions when my friends and I were able to get together. Whenever there was a full moon, we'd sit out on the path around the building and sing. Sometimes one of the Japanese guards would come out to watch us. Dressed only in his vest and shorts, he'd sit on a bench a short distance away – a plank between two stumps – and listen to us. He didn't bother us or ask us to quieten down. He would just sit there, looking slightly wistful. I wonder if he had children of his own somewhere and the sound of our voices brought back happy memories of spending time with his family before the war.

37

THE 'RIFF RAFF'

The incident with the rings at Changi was a valuable lesson for me in the all-pervasive power of social class in British society.

Prior to our internment, our family had never really mixed with the British expat community. In Johor Bahru, my friends were Malay, Chinese and Indian. Until the Curtis family arrived, we had been the only white people in our village. We knew nothing of the elite colonial life that many of the women in the camp had been used to. Now we were finding out that, even in captivity, class was a serious issue for those raised in the British Empire. Those women who had been 'senior ranking wives' outside the camp were determined to retain their status inside.

At Sime Road, our family had been billeted in Hut 16. The senior ranking wives, such as Lucy Marguerite Montgomery a.k.a. Lady Thomas, wife of Shenton Thomas, the former Straits Settlements Governor, and Lady Heath, wife of General Sir Basil Heath, commander of the 5th Indian Division at the time of the capitulation, were on the other side of the women's camp in Hut 10.

The women of Hut 10 took it in turns to act as camp

leaders, speaking on all our behalf to the Japanese. The leader was chosen via ballot, but to be on the ballot, you had to be one of the chosen few to begin with. It didn't seem to occur to them that we might choose a leader by a more democratic process. A leader from Hut 16, perhaps? Class trumped all. We came to understand that just as in Singapore before the occupation, where the upper and lower classes did not mix, there was an invisible line in the sand between our two huts that we simply did not cross. Though they were in the same camp, Hut 16 and Hut 10 might as well have been worlds apart.

Yet we – Mum, me, Mary, George and Peter – didn't really fit in anywhere. We weren't nearly posh enough to be in Hut 10 – since the incident with the rings, we were in no doubt that the ladies of Hut 10 considered our family to be riff-raff – but we were in the minority in Hut 16 too, where the majority of the women were ethnically Chinese or Eurasian. We were the only English family in Hut 16 (there were only eight white English children in the whole camp). Certain people referred to me and my siblings as 'half-breeds'. Similarly scorned was Mrs Ismael, a British woman who had married a Malay prince. Her husband might have been royalty to the Malays, but to the women of Hut 10, Mrs Ismael's marriage had not improved her status one bit. At the same time, it held her apart from the Hut 16 crowd.

It was the women of Hut 10 who decided that at Sime Road, my mother would have to work as a cook for the Japanese. Working as a cook doesn't sound too bad, until you realise that this particular position involved rising before four o'clock in the morning to chop wood to make a fire before the cooking started. The Japanese guards would just drop whole tree trunks next to the kitchen hut and expect Mum to get on with it, chopping the trunks into logs small enough for the grate. It was strange that they left her with an axe to do that with. Perhaps they decided she was too weak to be dangerous. Then there were the enormous metal woks for rice and tapioca to lug around and clean. Make no mistake, this was hard, physical labour.

Being a camp cook was no kind of privilege. Our mother's lowly status in the eyes of the Japanese was reflected in the fact that, even though the place where she laid her cooking fire was just a few feet from Hut 16, she was not allowed to take the direct path there since the direct path would have taken her past the guard's hut. So that she didn't disturb them, she had to take a long and convoluted route around half the camp, involving a rickety 'Chinese ladder' made of bamboo poles lashed together with string, to make sure that she stayed out of sight. The one good thing about Mum's new job was that she was able to give me the odd bit of charcoal, with which I would write on the path behind the hut. One day I used the charcoal to try to teach some of the younger children long division, but we were spotted by a guard and got into trouble.

While the Japanese guards remained relatively well-fed, by now we internees were on starvation rations. Every day we ate our rice boiled to the consistency of glue. The only flavourings came from scraps of rotten fish or the odd leaf or two. Salt was precious. From month to month, even the amount of rice we had been given was reduced again and again.

There was little chance that my mother would be able to steal much food as she cooked for the guards – it was all strictly accounted for – but she soon developed a strategy so that she could sneak just a little rice out. While she was cooking, she always let the rice toast on the bottom, so that some of it stuck. Then, while pretending to be cleaning the pots, she would set aside the toasted rice so that she could later pass it on to the camp's most sickly inmates and smallest children. She also preserved some of the rice water to give to me and my siblings, though this would eventually cause problems of its own.

One woman in particular was very grateful for Mum's cleverness. Mrs Hogg was an American. She lived on the posh side of the camp in a small hut which she had to herself. During the first few months at Sime Road she developed beriberi.

There are two types of beriberi: dry and wet. The symptoms of dry beriberi included muscle weakness and tingling of the arms and legs. Wet beriberi affects the cardio-vascular system, causing shortness of breath, swelling of the lower legs and an increased heart rate. Mrs Hogg had a particularly severe case of wet beriberi. Her heart was failing. It could no longer pump the blood around her body efficiently and she had terrible water retention, which made her swell up like a balloon. It got so bad that fluid even leaked from the ends of her fingers. Everyone expected that Mrs Hogg would die but Mum would not give up on her.

The only way to keep Mrs Hogg well was by feeding her greenery but there was none of that in our rations. Mum and I found a way around it. Each day, I would fetch Mrs Hogg's tin, in which she used to collect her food, and bring it to Mum, who would fill it with boiling water and whatever she could spare from the bottom of the guards' rice pot. As I carried it back to Mrs Hogg's hut, I would pretend that I could feel an insect crawling on my leg. That would give me an excuse to stop and bend down as I passed through the vegetable patches. While engaged in the pretence of getting rid of a bug, I would quickly pick some sweet potato leaves and pop them into Mrs Hogg's can. I would sneak this mixture to Mrs Hogg after lights out each night. Thankfully, this ensured that Mrs Hogg got just enough of the vitamins she needed to survive.

38

MAGGOTS AND SNAILS

Beriberi wasn't the only illness affecting our camp. Many other diseases caused by malnutrition or poor hygiene were increasingly common among the internees at Sime Road.

The conditions in the camp were very unsanitary and we no longer had the relief of those occasional trips to the sea to wash away the grime and all the nasty creatures that were attracted by it. The showers at Sime Road were beautiful – they had been built for RAF officers, after all – but the water was erratic and only came on from time to time. If you were working in the fields and the call came that 'water's on', by the time you got all the way to the shower block, it would inevitably have been turned off again.

When it rained, the makeshift lavatories overflowed and you had to walk through filthy water filled with maggots to get to the loo. The maggots would cling to you. They were very difficult to wash off.

When you had dysentery, which we all had practically all the time – sometimes so bad that it ran down our legs – the moment you heard the water had been turned on, you would grab a tin can or whatever came to hand and run to get whatever water you could. With soap a long distant memory and rags so precious, sometimes the only thing we had with which to clean ourselves was a leaf. There was nothing to be done about it. It was the way we had to live.

We were ravaged night and day by malaria-carrying mosquitoes. We had boils under our arms all the time. Our hair was full of nits and we couldn't cut our finger or toenails because we weren't allowed to have scissors. The worst thing for me was the boils I got on my kneecaps from working in the soil. They were so painful that sometimes I could hardly bend my knees to walk. The camp doctors couldn't do anything to help except try to cauterise them with that old heated-up knife blade.

We all had tapeworms and roundworm. We were absolutely full of lice. My brother Peter had it worst. He was very fair-skinned, got sunburnt easily and was always covered in sores that would get infested with maggots. We would have to dig them out for him. Mary made Peter a sort of scraper from a piece of coconut bark to help make the job less horrible. The malnutrition and severe skin problems that Peter developed in camp would affect him for the rest of his life.

There was no respite from biting insects when we were in bed either. At Changi, the bed bugs had been relatively easy to catch and kill as the concrete walls in the cells left them with nowhere to hide. At Sime Road, they lived in the wooden floor, where we couldn't get at them. All we could do was wait until they crawled out at night and had a free for all – feasting on our blood. We got our own back if they went into the sacking we used as bedding though. During the day we would lay the sacking out in the sun and the fierce red ants would eat the bugs, meaning we had clean – or at least relatively cleaner – sacking to use at bedtime.

We were a little more discriminating than the ants when it came to eating bugs and other nasties, but only just. In interviews after the war, Mrs Mulvany recalled having been made to eat rat meat during her solitary confinement. I don't remember that but I do know that my friends and I got so hungry that at one point, we ate grasshoppers. We'd fight over who got to them first. One day we even tried to eat the snails that crawled around the Sime Road gardens. We did our best to clean them – rubbing them in sand in an attempt to make them less slimy, as we had no fire to cook them on – but they still tasted horrible and now they were gritty to boot. We couldn't bear to swallow them. We just wanted something to chew on. It was a terrible experience and not one we wanted to repeat. All the same, by the end of the war, there were very few insects or other creatures that dared come anywhere near us, lest they end up in someone's mouth.

With all of us feeling so very hungry all the time, it became harder and harder to maintain the decorum and mealtime manners of which we had been so proud when we were first taken prisoner in 1942.

At Sime Road, we would reserve our places in the queue for food using our plates. One day, knocking off from the match factory for lunch, I put my tin down in place but then briefly left the queue to go to the loo. I returned to discover that an older woman had kicked my plate out of the way and taken my spot. When I protested at her cheek, she smacked me and I'm afraid I smacked her right back. I got into terrible trouble with Mum over my reaction but ultimately I think Mum understood the pressure we were all under as we pushed on through a third year in captivity.

39

'SHE'LL PULL THROUGH'

I got malaria very badly while we were at Sime Road. While I lay on a bed made of planks in the hospital hut, shaking and delirious and drifting in and out of consciousness, my mother heard some other prisoners gossiping that the guards had commanded them to prepare my coffin. She was furious and railed against them, telling them, 'You won't need that – she'll pull through.'

Though in Singapore we did have plenty of cinchona trees – fever trees – from the bark of which came quinine, a very effective treatment for malaria, I don't remember being given any medication at all. All I could do was ride the fever out.

Mum nursed me every step of the way, refusing to leave my side until I was well again. As she had promised, I did pull through. I owe Mum my life, as do so many other people who were inside Sime Road. But I found myself back in the hospital again not long afterwards.

One of my teeth had been giving me a lot of trouble. It was starting to get to the point that the swelling that had developed around it was pressing on the nerves in my face and making it hard for me to hear so it was decided that I would have to have it out. One of the doctors would do the job.

Of course there was no local anaesthetic in camp. Instead I gripped the side of the chair as the doctor grabbed the tooth in a pair of pliers and tugged until I felt the sickening sensation of the tooth's roots pulling free. With the tooth out, the doctor plugged the hole left behind with a piece of rag, telling me that I was to bite down upon it until the bleeding stopped.

The problem was, the bleeding did not stop. As the blood continued to pour from my mouth, the doctor realised that I was haemorrhaging.

As the doctor tried desperately to stem the bleeding, I thought I felt the spectre of death draw near. I was so frightened. I was sure that this must be the end. By the time the doctor managed to get the haemorrhaging under control, I had lost so much blood that I must have looked half-dead. I was carried to a bed in the hospital.

Over the next few days, my face turned black with bruising from where the doctor had had to press hard against my cheek to pull the tooth out. To stop the bleeding from starting up again, my head had to be wedged between two sacks of sand to keep it still. I couldn't even move my eyes. I remember trying to follow a shadow on the wall. I was desperate when I couldn't do it. I hated to feel so helpless. I had never liked to be in a position where I relied on other people to dress and undress me.

While I was in my sick bed, a group from the men's camp

was allowed into the women's section to perform a show. They set up just outside the hospital hut. Concerts were not always guaranteed to happen. The Japanese would often cancel them at the last minute if things were going badly for them in the war. When that happened, but a show was later allowed to go ahead, the privilege would be bitter sweet, because we would worry that it meant things were going well for the Japanese again.

This particular show did go ahead. Listening to the men singing, but unable to go and watch them, I felt like one of the loneliest people in the world. However, after the men went back to their camp, someone delivered a hand-drawn card to my bedside, drawn by a young man called Tommy Ryan who had befriended my brother Peter and thus heard that my birthday was coming up. It's a beautiful card, decorated with pixies, an owl in a tree and a glow-worm. I still have it to this day.

I was in the camp hospital for two weeks. Though it didn't feel like it at the time, I knew I had been lucky. There were many people who didn't make it. Strangely, though the Japanese seemed quite happy to watch us starve to death or die of easily preventable diseases, they were very superstitious about the rituals that accompany dying. Like the Chinese, the Japanese practised ancestor worship and thought that one should always treat the dead with the utmost respect (though how this fitted with the heads on the bridge, I do not know).

During the occupation, the Japanese always allowed

military personnel who died in the prison camps to be buried with full military honours. On our side of the camp at Sime Road, we had a coffin which was used for the funerals of all who died there. It wasn't a proper coffin. The Japanese didn't want to waste too much wood. It only had sides and a lid. No bottom. The body of the deceased was laid directly on the cart on which the coffin was placed. Burials were done at night. After the body went into the ground, the coffin would be retrieved from the grave and carefully kept until the next time. Thank goodness, our family never had to use it.

40

THE COMFORT WOMEN

If our family's experience of class prejudice and the unkind judgement of the 'high-ranking' women within the camp was bad, there were others who had it even worse. There was always a lot of gossip around the huts, usually about those women who had been mistresses to expat men before the war. Many of the expat wives looked down upon them, though by now we were all of us sorry, ragged creatures and you would have thought it made sense to treat each other more kindly. No. It seemed that even when living in such terrible conditions, there were people who could still find the energy to make someone else's life a little unhappier.

There was a small hut, almost at the camp's perimeter fence, that was occupied by two women who didn't mingle with the rest of us. They were the most beautiful women in the camp and they provided certain services to the Japanese officers. There were never queues outside the hut. They only spent time with the most senior officers. I didn't really understand what it was the women were doing when they invited the men inside, but I do know I felt very envious when I passed by their hut and smelled the delicious food they were cooking – payment for their services. It was torture!

Other women did not manage to turn their beauty to their advantage in quite such a successful way. Our hut had a verandah around the outside. There slept a young Eurasian woman who was considered by some to be even lower than the camp prostitutes. The woman – let's call her Alice – was the daughter of Mrs Holland, who slept near us. Alice was a latecomer to the camp, having been allowed to live freely for much of the war. When she was finally interned, she brought her baby, whose father was a Japanese soldier, with whom she had been having a relationship.

We were all of us hungry all the time and understood the urge to 'make friends' with the Japanese for something more to eat, but when Alice arrived with her half-Japanese baby there was outrage. She was ostracised by most of the women in the camp and made to sleep outside. Her baby girl, so small and vulnerable, had to sleep out there with her. The verandah was completely open to the elements. When it rained, their bedding was soaked right through and they were always at the mercy of mosquitoes.

As a child, I wasn't entirely sure what Alice had done wrong and, to help her out, I would often offer to take the baby for a while so that she could get some rest. I had always enjoyed looking after babies – when we first arrived at camp, I'd looked after a baby called Buster. Now I jumped at the chance to look after this sweet little child. I would carry her around on my hip and try to amuse her. I loved having her in my arms and I'm sure it gave Alice a valuable opportunity to rest.

Though no-one ever said anything to me about it, there

were some in the camp who took it upon themselves to ask my mother why on earth she was allowing me to associate with a fallen woman and her child. My mother got fed up with the comments, which she felt were unnecessary and unhelpful, but she didn't ever stop me from looking after the baby. Regarding Alice and the 'comfort women' in their special hut, Mum's view was always 'each to their own'. Her Christian faith, and her own experience of the camp's grand ladies, had taught her not to be judgmental. When we were all struggling to survive from day-to-day, what was the point of making life more difficult for our fellow internees with no good reason?

The ladies who were so unkind to Alice and so judgmental of the comfort women always made sure to be there on Sunday morning when the vicar from the men's camp next door was allowed in to deliver the sacrament, but sometimes that looked less like Christianity than hypocrisy. Through witnessing such behaviour, my eyes were opened to the nastiness with which women can treat other women and I grew up pretty quickly. Meanwhile, Mum always made sure she saved a little bit of rice for the baby made to sleep on the verandah.

I think it was the way those 'high-ranking' ladies acted towards Mrs Holland's daughter and granddaughter that made Mum keep quiet when they asked everyone in the camp to add any food they had brought into a stock that would be distributed to those in need. Mum no longer trusted that the women who took it upon themselves to rule over us had our best interests at heart. She didn't see the food and other goods that had been handed in being shared out to the needy as promised so she kept the condensed milk and marmite she had brought from Uncle Tom's house for her own children. As soon as she saw one of us really suffering, she would open up a tin.

Mum often put herself in danger for us and for other vulnerable people in the camp. She always seemed to put herself last and was always very brave. She worked harder than anyone I knew. Then, one day, while on her way to her fire in the pouring rain – doubtless carrying something heavy at the time – she slipped on the rickety bamboo ladder and fell and in doing so, she put her shoulder out. The accident left her in terrible pain. But of course, she still had to work. She still had to rise before dawn to chop wood. I did as much as I could, getting up at 4.30 in the morning to help Mum lay the fire, but I still had my own work to do too.

Before her accident, Mum always wore her beautiful hair long – so long that she could sit on the ends. After she injured her shoulder, we had to cut it short for her – like a boy's – because she couldn't comb it by herself. My sister and I weren't able to comb it for her because we had to be in the shirt and match factories respectively. Mum's trusty Mason and Pearson brush had long since disappeared, lost or more likely stolen and bartered for food. It was sad to see Mum lose the crowning glory we had always known. It felt symbolic, somehow. Like Samson losing his hair and his strength.

41

CAUGHT IN THE ACT

We were all perpetually hungry and that hunger often drove us to take big risks. Back at Changi, my friend Eileen Harris and her family had been given a sleeping place next to a wire cage where the Japanese kept bananas. Eileen and I would spend hours trying to fish one of those bananas out with a piece of string.

At Sime Road, I remember once spotting a ripe paw-paw on a tall tree near our hut. We weren't meant to take any of the fruit from the trees that dotted the camp. It was strictly reserved for the Japanese soldiers. But one day my sister Mary and I decided that we were going to have that paw-paw regardless of the risk. When the coast was clear, Mary helped me to climb up into the tree, but I had only just got up there when we heard the footsteps of a guard approaching. Quick as a flash, Mary made a run for it back into the hut, leaving me stuck up the tree on my own, unable to do anything but stay as quiet and still as I could, hoping that the guard would not look up as he passed by underneath. I stayed successfully hidden until he was gone but it was an uncomfortably close shave.

Sometimes, at night my friends and I dared each other to steal food from the gardens at Sime Road – pumpkins, melons, that sort of thing. On nights when it was pouring with rain and dark, we would sit at the top of the storm drain, let go and slip all the way down. This was our fast route to the gardens around the guards' storehouse. I remember a time when, together with Eileen and Ozzie Hancock – we were 'the three musketeers' – I stole a type of melon. We'd kept an eye on it while it was growing and thought that it was ready to eat. It turned out that it wasn't. The unripe fruit blistered my mouth. With the evidence of what I'd been up to all over my face, I had to be kept in as much as possible until the sores healed, always remembering to cover my mouth in the presence of the Japanese guards.

I'm sure that Mum knew what my friends and I got up to by night – we were all so tightly packed into Hut 16, I couldn't have left without her noticing – but she didn't ever try to stop me. She must have known there was no point arguing about it. Arguing would only have drawn the guards' attention to what was going on which would have been bad news for all of us. Mum just wanted to be sure that we didn't take George with us. She just hoped that I was clever enough not to be caught. With our mothers turning a blind eye, my friends and I took bigger and bigger risks, until one terrible night in September '44, when it all went very wrong.

After the usual evening tenko out in the sandy yard, everyone went into the hut for the night. Eileen and her family had the spot next to ours on the floor. Our beds were just 24 inches apart. Once our mothers were safely sleeping, Eileen crept over to me and asked if I was going to go hunting for food with her and some other girls. They were new girls, slightly younger than we were, who had not been at Sime Road for long. I didn't know them well.

'Are you coming?' Eileen asked.

I don't know why that night felt different, but it did, and I told Eileen that I wouldn't be going with her. I was going to stay in the hut.

'Suit yourself then,' said Eileen.

The others – six of them altogether – sneaked out of the hut without me.

Having dodged the searchlights, the intrepid six went up to the hill where we grew crops. There the girls pulled up a row of tapioca six feet long. They thought they were being clever when they took off the roots – the only edible part of the plant – then replanted the stalks to make it look as if nothing had happened. But of course, without roots to supply them with water, the stalks quickly drooped and when they withered in the sun the following day, the Japanese wanted to know what had happened. It didn't take long for them to catch the girls who'd been involved. The guards made it clear that if no-one admitted to the crime, everybody would be punished. After that, they knew that the women of the camp would pressurise the culprits to come clean, or even turn the girls in themselves to avoid an unnecessary beating.

Hearing that Eileen and the others had been identified as the thieves, I was terrified for them. I couldn't believe how lucky I'd been that I had decided not to go with them when they pulled the tapioca up. But did I deserve to have got away with it when I'd been with Eileen on so many other occasions?

When my mother heard the other women talking about the girls who had been caught stealing, she asked me 'were you out last night too?' I couldn't lie to her. I said, 'Not last night, Mum. But every other time.' With a heavy sigh, Mum told me, 'Then you'll have to own up too.' There was a code of honour at stake.

Mum came with me to The Flying Dutchman, which was now the camp commandant's office. There I admitted to Dr Smallwood, the current commandant, that though I hadn't been in the gang that stole the tapioca, I had been with them on many occasions and wanted to own up to theft too. Without hesitation, Dr Smallwood batted the idea away, firmly telling me, 'No. You mustn't do that.'

'But I should be punished as well,' I said. 'If they are. I've stolen food in the past.'

'No,' she said again. 'We have enough problems on our hands. I don't want another one added. We don't have the medical supplies.'

It sounded heartless but Dr Smallwood knew, as my mother and I did, that the punishment meted out to the girls already caught would likely be physical and it could be brutal. Mum agreed with Dr Smallwood. There was no point in adding to the number of casualties the medical staff already had to deal with. So I listened to Dr Smallwood and kept my mouth shut.

The following day, the other girls received their punishment. They were made to kneel in the sun from morning until night. If they keeled over, they got the whip. Everyone was made to watch at some point during the day. But that wasn't all.

Eileen's father, who was in the men's camp, had somehow heard what was happening. When he protested at the harshness of the girls' treatment, the Japanese brought him over to our side and whipped him in front of us for daring to speak up. It was Blue Stocking who delivered the blows. Mr Harris was beaten so badly that he had to be carried back through the barbed wire.

The horrendous beatings had the desired effect. They made us all very wary. Eileen and I did not try to steal tapioca roots or anything else ever again.

Over the years I have often felt uneasy about the fact that I escaped punishment that day. I know that Dr Smallwood made a pragmatic decision. She knew she did not have the resources to treat the wounds she expected the girls to receive. Still, I have often felt that I should have been there, kneeling alongside my friends. I was very fortunate that the other girls seemed to understand my dilemma and were of the view that Dr Smallwood had made the right choice. What was the point of all of us being in pain? I had always admired Eileen for her courage. From then on, I admired her even more.

DAD AND PETER

As the weeks turned into months and the months turned into years, we wondered if our incarceration would ever end. We also wondered what had become of Dad. Getting news of him was harder than ever. Was he well? Was he keeping his spirits up? Then, suddenly, towards the end of the war – about four months before the liberation – we were told we would be allowed to meet our men folk in the middle ground between our two camps. We were incredibly excited at the prospect of seeing Dad again.

On the morning of the big day, we all tried to look our best – no mean feat when our clothes were rags and our skin was covered in sores. The guards led us to the meeting place and we waited for the men. When they appeared, my siblings and I straight away spotted our father but Dad was leaning heavily on a stick and he appeared not to be able to see us as we waved. We later learned that he had gone blind. My brother Peter ran over to Dad and led him to a nearby tree so that he might lean against it while we talked.

We found out that Dad had lost his sight through malnutrition and was being kept in a hut reserved for the sick and the old. He was able at least to tell us that Uncle Tom was in Changi too. Uncle Tom had always been so tall and thin, we wondered how he was coping on camp rations. We never found out what had become of his mistress, Auntie Amy.

Before we had been with our father for very long, we noticed some fruit fall. We were very attuned to such things by now. All our senses were directed towards finding food. My brother quickly picked it up and offered some to Dad. Knowing at once the danger Peter was putting himself in, Dad said, 'Just throw it down.' But Peter, desperately hungry as we all were, dared to take a bite. A Japanese guard immediately ran over and knocked Peter to the ground.

The family visit was cancelled at once. Though we pleaded with the guards to have mercy, the men were sent back to their camp while Peter was taken to the area where the men did PE and tied to a vaulting horse to be whipped. Peter fainted. Other prisoners pleaded for him to be let go. What was the point of continuing to flog him when he was unconscious? But the Japanese didn't relent. There was nothing we could do except be there to hold and comfort him when the beating was over.

The wounds Peter received that day were appalling. They turned into long pink scars that haunted Peter for the rest of his life. Even as an adult, he would never take his shirt off in front of other people, not even on the beach.

We all had a terrible time in camp but Peter had the worst of it by far. Our side of the camp was officially for women but when we first were interned, boy children were allowed to stay with their mothers until the age of 12. When they turned 12, they were taken away and put in with the men. At 12, some of the boys were ready to be away from their mothers, but as the war progressed (and perhaps because the Japanese knew it was not going their way), the age at which the boys were taken was suddenly lowered to 10. This change came in just in time to catch Peter, Gordon Shorthouse and their friends Jimmy Greenaway and Hugh Davidson.

It might have been bearable for Peter had our father been able to look after him once he arrived at the men's camp, but Dad was far too ill and my brother could not join him in the hut where Dad stayed with the other invalids. Fortunately, two men who had known our family before the occupation stepped in to take care of Peter in Dad's place.

Guy Mitchell and his friend Bob Roberts had both been barbers in Singapore. Guy had cut Peter's hair since he was a small child. Together with Bob, Guy took Peter under his wing and did his best to make sure that he was fed and happy. It involved no small risk. Guy cut the hair of the Japanese officers and, from time to time, he would be in their mess while they were eating. If they left scraps, he would steal them and bring them back for my brother. He would also rummage through the guards' bins for anything useful. In that way, he kept Peter alive.

Though he was only 10 and desperately weak through malnourishment, the Japanese put Peter to work on the land with the adults. It wasn't long before he developed ulcers, terrible things. He was covered in maggots where flies had landed on the sores and laid their eggs. In a desperate attempt to keep the flies off, Guy found a piece of old mosquito net in one of the bins and hung it from a tree to make a sort of tent for Peter to sit beneath.

Peter was very fair and small. He'd always been little for his age. In Johor Bahru, his nickname was 'White Monkey' because he was so blond his hair seemed to shine. He was the only fair one in the family and Mum and Dad had always taken special care of his skin. Out in the fields all day, with no shirt to cover him, Peter soon got badly sun-burned. When one of the men called the Japanese guard over and tried to tell him that Peter needed to be in the shade because his skin was stripped raw by the sun, the guard just laughed and urinated on Peter's back. That was the vile man's only comment on the situation. The same guard liked to come up behind Peter while he was bending over in the fields, and kick him between the legs.

By the time the war ended, Peter was in a mess, an absolute mess. He was picked on by the Japanese guards all the time. As a direct result of his mistreatment, he spent most of his adult life fighting skin cancer and was never able to have children.

Mum was devastated by having to watch Peter join the men. As his 10th birthday approached, we had all been filled with quiet dread. Once he was gone away from us, Mum quickly went downhill. She was filled with anguish at the thought that she could no longer care for him as she wanted to. All of us missed him terribly.

I remember one day that Peter came right up to the wire that separated the women's camp from the men's. He just wanted to catch a glimpse of one of us, to hear some words of comfort. How lonely he must have been, separated from me, Mary, George and Mum and with Dad too ill to take care of him.

I saw Peter at the fence and though I was as desperate to talk to him as he must have been to talk to me, I knew I had to tell him to go back. If the guards saw him, there would be trouble

'Go back,' I hissed at him. 'You've got to go back.'

It was for his own sake and I was sure that he knew I was right to shoo him off but my heart broke as he turned and walked away, shoulders sagging and head down. It was such cruelty, to keep a boy so young away from his family.

Christmas 1944 was an especially miserable time. The camp commandant promised that we would have a Christmas feast. There would be bread and pork, he said.

You can imagine the excitement. And you can probably imagine the disappointment when Christmas dinner arrived and we discovered that the 'bread' was just a dry stick made of two thumbs of mashed-up corn – the same as usual – and that there were only seven tiny cubes of pork floating in the water that had to be shared between all of us. It was a far cry from the Christmas feasts we'd had back in Johor Bahru.

But we had to keep our hopes up. We had to keep believing that one day the Japanese would be defeated and those glorious Johor Bahru Christmases would come again. One day we would sit around a table with Peter and Dad and laugh and be happy and our internment would be nothing but a memory. That had to be the truth.

43

THE PUSHBACK

Unbeknown to us prisoners, by 1944 the tide of war was turning in the Allies' favour.

An attempted Japanese invasion of India had gone badly and by May they were withdrawing, with huge casualties. Meanwhile in Europe, on June 4th, the Allies captured Rome. Two days later, they launched the D-Day Landings in Normandy, beginning the pushback in France. Throughout the summer and autumn, the US forces had made headway in the Philippines. While we were enduring a miserable Christmas at Sime Road, the British Fourteenth Army was fighting in Burma. In January 1945, the US landed forces in the Philippines and in February, they landed on the island of Iwo Jima, one of Japan's territories in Micronesia.

The Battle Of Iwo Jima was one of the bloodiest battles in the Pacific War, lasting for more than five weeks. There were enormous numbers of casualties on both sides, but the American forces prevailed. Meanwhile, the British took Meiktila and Mandalay in Burma.

The Allied Forces were making serious headway and it wasn't long before fighter planes started to fly over Singapore again. This time, however, we were glad to see them. Sometimes, they flew right over the camp. We'd run to the top of the hill to get a closer look. Were they ours? We children were sure they were English planes and waved like crazy but the adults stopped us.

'Be careful, they might be Japanese,' the grown-ups said.

Having lived under Japanese rule for almost three years, we heeded the warnings. We didn't doubt that a Japanese pilot might open fire on us for daring even to look up. But they were Allied Fighter planes, we were certain, and we felt more hopeful than ever that help was on its way. We were glad to know that the Allies were bombing Singapore, even when the bombs fell perilously close to the walls of the camp.

Victory in Europe edged closer. On April 30th 1945, Hitler took his own life in his Fuhrerbunker in Berlin. On May 8th, henceforth to be known as VE Day, Germany signed the unconditional surrender. With the war in Europe over, the Allies would be able to turn their full attention to the Far East.

By July, the Japanese in Singapore must have known that it wouldn't be long before the Allied Forces got the better of them but they weren't about to raise the white flag. That was not the Japanese way. Surrender was not a word in their vocabulary.

Still at Sime Road, things were changing in subtle ways. To begin with, there was a change in personnel. The guards we had known for months suddenly disappeared to be replaced by others. Then the Japanese ended the manufacture of uniforms and closed down the camp's match factory. Those of us that had been employed there were instead tasked with digging a tunnel, tall enough to walk into and long enough to fit many people inside, into the side of the hill behind the huts.

Officially, we were digging a tunnel for storage. We had to pull up all the tapioca that had been planted on the hill to make space. Because we had to dig so hard, we were given an extra tablespoon of rice. But as we worked, a rumour went around that we were digging our own graves. If the Japanese were going to die, they were going to take us prisoners with them. We heard that when the tunnel was finished, the guards would march all 2700 of us in there and throw a bomb in after us. They would rather see us perish than see us liberated.

Who knows how close we came to the end. Later we would discover that the Japanese had already earmarked a day for our deaths. But on August 6th 1945, the Americans dropped an atomic bomb − the first of its kind − on the Japanese city of Hiroshima. Three days later, they did the same in Nagasaki. The detonations shocked the world, but they ended the war in the Far East. The Japanese capitulated on August 14th 1945.

PART
FIVE

Liberation

*"My hair – uncut for years – was wild and full of nits.
I was embarrassed to be seen like that by the soldiers,
who looked so clean and healthy when they arrived."*

1945 – 1949

44

BREAD AND BUTTER

The Japanese announced their surrender the day after the capitulation (the formal surrender would be signed on September 2nd) but it would be a while before we internees found out what had happened. The good news eventually arrived in the form of hundreds of leaflets, dropped from allied planes. As the leaflets began to flutter down over Sime Road, we all rushed to grab them. We children were pushing each other out of the way, trying to get one as they drifted down. I still have the leaflet I picked up to this day. The war was over! To see it in writing was wonderful.

As well as confirming the end of the fighting, the leaflets outlined arrangements for the welfare of prisoners going forward. For the moment, we were told we were to stay put in the camp, under the control of the Japanese guards. There was nowhere else for us to go until the Allies were able to set in place plans for an evacuation. But neither was there anything for us to eat where we were. The Japanese could no longer feed us or themselves.

But then the Allies started dropping food along with the leaflets. The first thing we had was a loaf of bread but that was to be shared between 32 people, which was no easy task, when none of us had a knife with which to cut it. The next day they dropped butter. Though we had barely a scrap of bread to put it on, the Allies dropped the best part of half a pound of butter per person! We ate it by the handful. You can imagine what happened next. After more than three years of starvation rations, we had the most awful dysentery ever from the richness. I had the runs until we were sent back to England, many weeks later.

It was only after the Allies dropped the butter and we'd eaten it, that they dropped leaflets warning us not to eat too much because our bodies wouldn't be able to handle it. That came too late! We did hear afterwards that some of the prisoners liberated from Japanese camps in the Philippines had stuffed themselves with every bit of food they could lay their hands on and died as a consequence.

The Allies were determined to be more careful with us but their plan that the Japanese guards would keep control of the camp in the interim did not work out. To have lost the war was a huge dishonour and the Japanese guards could see no way to redeem themselves. One by one, they left their posts and went to commit hara-kiri or seppuku – a form of ritualised suicide by disembowelment, traditionally practised by the Samurai. Many of the guards chose to do it at the camp's reservoir. Perhaps that was a final act of defiance, polluting the water source.

Thus we internees were left alone, without food (except for the few things that the Allies had dropped) and with no means to buy any. But the disappearance of the guards did mean that we were able to walk freely around the camp at last, to venture further afield in search of something to eat or things we could barter in exchange for a few scraps. Mum instructed Mary, George and me to look for shoes. Most of us were barefoot by now – I had long since grown out of my school shoes – and our feet were cracked and painful.

I went scavenging with my old friend Eileen. We crept into the Japanese officers' quarters and rifled through the drawers of the desks there. We were delighted when we found a packet of balloons. We each took half and went back to our mothers. I thought Mum would be thrilled to see what I'd found but when her eyes widened and her cheeks went pink, I guessed that something was amiss. What Eileen and I thought were balloons, were actually rubber condoms. Mary was so embarrassed that she told me she was going to pretend she didn't know me.

Eileen and I set out again. With so many people hunting for anything they could sell, there wasn't much left to find, until we went into the camp's Japanese garden, behind the house where the officers had lived.

That Japanese garden was a beautiful place. It had been built by POWs at the beginning of the war. It had elegant flower beds and rock pools, dotted with water lilies. In the middle of so much destruction and desperation, the garden still seemed strikingly serene. Until we noticed that it wasn't only lilies that were floating in the water.

The garden had become a popular spot for the Japanese

guards to commit hara-kiri. They had positioned themselves so that they would fall into the pond as they died on their own swords and daggers. Now flies hovered above the bloated corpses, filling the air with their sickening buzz. The smell of death was unmistakable, taking me right back to the days before Singapore fell, when the blood of the dying filled the storm drains.

As we stood at the side of the pond, Eileen and I shared a glance. It's a mark of how dehumanised she and I had become through our experiences in camp, that when I suggested we check the officers' dead bodies for valuables, Eileen didn't flinch. Nor did she immediately dismiss the idea.

'Why not?' she shrugged.

We didn't recognise any of the men in the water. Perhaps that made it easier. Silently, we went about our grisly business.

For obvious reasons, we didn't want to get into the pond so, working together, we managed to pull one of the officers onto dry land. As we did so, one of his arms came away in our hands. Covering our noses, we rolled the dead man over and went through his uniform, quickly emptying his pockets. We took his pistol. We could almost certainly get money for that. There wasn't much else. But then we noticed the dead soldier's teeth – bared in death's rictus grin – were filled with gold. Gold was something we definitely knew we could swap for something to eat.

'What should we do?' Eileen asked me.

We both knew we had to get those teeth.

'Is it wrong?' I wondered aloud.

Eileen shrugged again. I shrugged too.

It might have been wrong, but as far as we were concerned, it was simply a matter of survival. If we didn't get that gold, I was sure that someone else would. We needed to eat and, truth be told, we had no real feelings about what we were doing at all. Not guilt, not sadness, not fear, not disgust. We felt nothing.

I found a stick and we set to work. Decay had made the dead man's teeth loose in his gums. They came out surprisingly easily and it wasn't long before we had a small handful. This was real treasure. We headed back to the hut to find Mum. I thought she would be delighted. The gold in my fist would buy a lot of bread. But…

'Olga!'

Mum was horrified.

'What on earth have you done?'

Mum took the teeth from me and immediately got rid of them, burying them in the dirt as quickly as she could. She was heartbroken that our years in captivity had reduced us to such things. She made me promise that no matter how hungry we were, I would never take anything from a dead man again.

I kept my promise.

45

THE CAVALRY ARRIVES

A couple of days after Eileen and I took those gold teeth, we were still waiting for liberation when a US army jeep briefly drove in through the camp gates. There was only one soldier on board. Pulling the jeep to a standstill in the yard, he stood up in his seat, looked around at the half-dead women and children shuffling about the huts, shook his head and drove straight off again.

When proper relief finally arrived at the camp, we must have looked a right state. For a long time, we'd had no soap with which to wash ourselves or our clothes. We were all skin and bone but had the bloated bellies characteristic of malnutrition. I had beriberi from drinking all the tapioca water. My waist measured 42 inches yet my limbs were horribly withered. I looked more like a football with matchsticks for legs than a human girl. My hair – uncut for years – was wild and full of nits. I was embarrassed to be seen like that by the soldiers, who looked so clean and healthy when they arrived.

The Allies were serious about making sure that we didn't eat too much too quickly. The Japanese were gone but now we had new guards around the camp to keep the local people from getting in. They were worried that the locals would give us gifts or try to sell us food that might lead to us overeating.

Altogether we were in Sime Road for a further five weeks after the Japanese capitulation. The adults tried to make sure we stuck to some kind of routine to stop everything falling apart.

We still had to queue for meals and though we were allowed to visit the men's camp and vice versa we had a curfew. We had to be back in the women's camp by six. Some women, like Freddy Bloom, did sneak out to stay with their husbands overnight but we wouldn't see Dad until we boarded the ship to sail back to England.

During this time, the adults were each given a small amount of money, which became known as the 'Freedom Fiver'. We learned that the non-Europeans who had been interned were given only half that amount, which caused no small amount of anguish.

While we were still in the camp, Allied dignitaries came to visit. Among them were Admiral Lord Louis Mountbatten, Commander-In-Chief, South Asian Command, and, on a separate occasion his wife Lady Mountbatten. They brought with them food parcels and much anticipated news of people back home. I somehow missed both visits.

Eventually, we were allowed to leave Sime Road. At last we were properly free and in a neat reversal of fortune, many of the Japanese guards and Kenpetai who had made our lives at Changi and Sime Road so miserable, were arrested and found themselves behind the bars at Changi Prison. The hated Tommy Naga was among them.

The reputation of expats in Singapore is not a good one, but I think it says something about the very real relationships we had with the local people, that when the Allies finally opened the gates of Sime Road, we walked out to be greeted by Dad's driver Moktaya, our former amah and Kahboom, who had tended our gardens in Johor Bahru. They were all anxiously waiting to see if we had survived and when they saw that we had, they were keen to take up their roles at our house once more.

There were many people in need of work. The locals in Johor Bahru may not have been interned, but they had not come through the occupation unscathed. They suffered from terrible food shortages. When the Japanese invaded the peninsula, they had churned up the rice fields on their way, causing the harvest to fail. Later harvests were confiscated to feed the Japanese army.

Though we were glad to see our old friends, Dad had to explain that we were not in a position to give anyone any work. We didn't even know if our old house was still standing. Neither would our old friends be able to come back to England with us.

The British authorities had offered us the chance to go back to Britain or to Australia. Dad, having spent much of his youth in Australia, was keen to go there, but Mum thought differently. She had not seen her side of the family since 1927, when she returned from looking after her grandmother in Cambridgeshire to Singapore to marry Dad. After much discussion, Mum won. We would all be going 'home' with her to England.

46

THE SS ALMANZORA

We could not leave for England right away. All of us had malaria and had to be dosed up on quinine and atabrine before we were even allowed onto a ship. When we finally boarded the SS Almanzora on October 15th 1945 (this time we were definitely on the list) we found that the ship was so crowded with British internees and POWs heading home there was nowhere to sleep but on deck. With only rough army blankets to cover us, we made our beds beneath the stars.

We had brought nothing with us from the camp but the precious photograph album that Mum had carried with her from Johor Bahru, more than three years before. Those photographs were proof that we had once been an ordinary family, living an ordinary life – happy and free. We hoped that we were about to start a wonderfully ordinary life again.

The voyage back to Britain was no luxury cruise. We had to wash with sea water and during the day, we were given the task of looking out for floating mines. Meanwhile the SS Almanzora was so old, she barely seemed sea-worthy. Overloaded with passengers, she sat so low in the water that she looked as though she was already half-sunk before we even left port. But on board, we were treated with a kindness that we hadn't felt in a very long time.

We were properly fed and gradually nursed back to health. We were all in a bit of a state. Our feet were very beaten up. While we were still in Sime Road, after the end of the war but before the Allies came to fetch us, Mum had bartered with Mordecai, one of the Jewish men in the men's camp, to try to get some shoes for me. He'd found her a pair. They were blue leather with a white tongue and they cost the equivalent of $200! Mum had to give him her last piece of jewellery, a string of beads she had managed to keep hidden through all that time in the camps, to be able to pay for them, only to find that when she got hold of them, they were too tight for me. I couldn't wear them. Fortunately, she was able to give them to Peter when we were at last reunited.

As well as being without shoes, neither had we been able to clean our teeth properly for three years. My teeth were in awful condition. Because I'd been eating nothing but soft, pappy rice for so long, the gums had grown over some of them. They needed to be cut away. It was a huge relief to have a toothbrush again – we had been given those – but it would take a skilful dentist to repair the damage caused by so many months of neglect.

Our long journey back to England took us via Colombo in Ceylon (now Sri Lanka). There we were met by volunteers from the local Red Cross who gave us donated bits and pieces. I was given a pair of women's army shoes and two pairs of socks, which I would definitely need when we docked in Southampton. Then, when we reached Aiden, someone gave me a little dressing gown and a new dress. At Port Said, another kind person gave me some little bloomers and two liberty bodies, to which you could attach stockings.

I have a photograph of me with Peter and George on board the ship. Playing under the watchful eye of the Red Cross nurses, we look like any happy group of children. We loved still having our friends around. Eileen Harris was on the same ship as us. But though we had left the camp, the camp had not entirely left us.

George in particular had terrible nightmares. He would wake in tears every night, screaming 'don't put me in the box! Don't put me in the box!' We worked out that the box he was referring to was the old packing case that had held our most precious belongings in Hut 16. With Peter gone to the men's camp, and me, Mum and Mary at work, George would be left alone in the hut, in sole charge of our patch of sacking and that box. We knew that if the box was left unguarded, other women in the camp would take the opportunity to go through our belongings. Desperation had made thieves of even the most honest people.

George would sit in the box to protect our things and sometimes he would have to be in there for hours. The responsibility had obviously weighed very heavily upon him. Far more heavily than we had ever known. George took after our father and looked tough, but inside he was quite timid and shy.

We later found out that while George had grown during the camp, his organs had merely stretched. This had created pockets around his heart and kidneys that made him prone to infection. He was unwell for most of his life.

Despite what he'd been through, Peter retained his cheerful nature, and his physical scars – from the sunburn and the beatings he received in the men's camp – were slowly healing but they would never go away. They made him too self-conscious to strip off and jump into the sea with the rest of us children. He insisted on keeping a shirt and trousers on at all times.

Meanwhile Dad was still unable to see properly, though it was hoped that having access to the food and vitamins he needed would start to make a difference. Every sea mile and ship meal brought us a little nearer to health.

As we sailed closer to Europe, the weather grew colder and the skies were more grey than blue. Landing in Southampton at the end of October, we wondered what we had come 'home' to. It wasn't home to me, Mary, Peter and George. We had never been to Britain before. Home to us would always be Malaya. I don't know if I cried, but I must have wanted to as I stepped onto British soil for the first time in my life at 13 years old.

47

'YOU HAD IT EASY'

Having docked in Southampton at long last, we travelled onwards to London by train. There we were going to stay with Mum's younger sister Maud and her family for a couple of days. It wasn't a comfortable experience. We were still covered in sores and our English relatives were worried that we might have brought some kind of lice or nits from the camp, so we were made to sleep in the lean-to shed that backed onto the house.

Our relatives weren't entirely wrong to think that we were still carrying the infestations we'd picked up in Changi and Sime Road. I remember being horrified when I used a toilet that wasn't just a hole in the ground for the first time, only to discover that I was full of worms. Until that moment, I had never really thought about them. Now that I knew they were inside me, I wouldn't be happy until they were gone. We couldn't afford to see a doctor. This was in the days before the National Health Service. Instead, Dad made me drink some strong beer to kill them off. Luckily it seemed to work.

It was a strange time. Though they must have known something of what we had been through, my aunt's family continually assured us that we knew nothing of war. They'd had to live through the Blitz and put up with rationing, they told us. They forgot that we had been bombed in Singapore and Johor Bahru too. And as if their experience of food shortages was anything like ours! They made no effort whatsoever to understand just how bad our war had been.

When Mum's aunt called us to the table on our first night there, I took a bit of butter and put it on the side of my plate. It caused an uproar. 'You can't just do that!' my great-aunt told me. 'There's no butter to be wasted here!'

I didn't understand the fuss, not knowing at the time that our relations were having to feed us from their own rations while we waited for our ration books to arrive. I suppose that makes their complaining a little more understandable.

Two days later, Mum's uncle managed to rent us a terraced cottage in Swavesey, near the village where Mum had grown up. It was far from lovely. In many ways, being there was like going back to camp. There was no running water apart from a tap in the garden, and the toilet was just a bucket outside. We were actually shocked at how primitive it was.

In Malaya before the war, everyone had proper bathrooms. We were used to bathing twice a day. Our English cousins had a bath night once a week. It was completely against our way of life.

When we first arrived, we were invited to the shire hall in Cambridge and there we were each presented with a bottle of 'Radio Malt' – a horrible gooey spread like Nutella, only made of malt for the Vitamin B. It tasted completely vile but it was supposed to be good for us. That was all the help we got from the council there.

Luckily, many of my mother's people had farms so we did get some extra milk. We were also given coupons for clothes and food but they forgot we didn't have any money. My father's bank account was with the Hong Kong and Shanghai Bank in Singapore. There were some kind people who tried to help us but it seemed that everyone in England was hard-up too. Mum turned to her needleworking skills again. She would go to the market in Cambridge and get odds and ends of material from which she made us clothes. I had a coat made from an old army blanket. It was a good coat but worn over my thin white cotton dress, it must have marked me out as a refugee. People crossed the street to avoid us.

Everyone who had been interned in the Far East received a letter, on Buckingham Palace notepaper, from King George VI and the Queen. The letter began, 'The Queen and I bid you a very warm welcome home.

'Through all the great trials and sufferings which you have undergone at the hands of the Japanese, you and your comrades have been constantly in our thoughts.

'We know from the accounts we have already received how heavy those sufferings have been. We know also that these have been endured by you with the highest courage.

'With all our hearts, we hope that your return from captivity will bring you and your families a full measure of happiness, which you may long enjoy together.'

But it seemed to me that our fellow British citizens resented having more mouths to feed when they were still living with the fall-out of more than five years of war with Germany.

That warm welcome of which the King spoke was only on paper.

The way we were treated by some of the people we met when we lived in England in those post-war years has left me with memories that make my heart go out to anyone arriving as a refugee in the UK now.

48

LETTERS FROM 'HOGGIE'

In the months immediately following our liberation, we lost touch with many of the people who had been with us in camp, as we dispersed to all corners of the world. I am sure there were many internees who didn't want to be reminded of the war years, who were happy, as our mother's relatives exhorted us, to try to forget all about it and get on with our lives. But we did hear from some of our old friends.

Mrs Hogg often wrote to my mother in the years post-liberation. Though she had been one of the grander ladies in the camp, she never forgot the risks my mother and I had taken to nurse her back to health when she was so ill with beriberi. Mrs Hogg's first letter, sent from India where she was convalescing in hospital, reveals the extent of the damage done to her body by malnutrition and just how much effort getting well again involved. And how much food!

She wrote, 'Have received 5 blood transfusions and 7 plasma transfusions and 3 to 5 injections every day of liver, iron, and all vitamins besides, many pills and capsules of all the latest and newest medicines, then I am on a 5,000 calorie high protein diet – get food 6 times a day and each time there is enough for three people but I eat it all. Lots of milk and egg nogs to drink besides all the good coffee that I want. I average six eggs a day, butter, cheese, lean meat, puddings and rich soups, chicken, fish and beautiful veg or fruit salads – they say it is my salvation that I can eat and like it.

'I weighed 82 lbs (without water) when I came and now I weigh 116 lbs. Can you believe it? My face is fat and full and I have my dimples as I did when I was a youngster. My yellow complexion is now gone and my cheeks and lips are very rosy red and my skin nice and white. All the swelling is gone from my legs but my abdomen is still very distended and I look as if I am about 9 months pregnant. My pet colonel calls it my 3 ½ year pregnancy and every so often they ask when I'm going to deliver. The nurses have been so sweet. They cut my hair and gave me a permanent. They are the new ones from America and you can do it yourself and it does not need electricity at all – then they comb it up the latest way – it looks very nice and you would never know me.

'Providence certainly was looking after me sending me here. My husband stayed here 2 weeks then he went by plane (3 ½ days) to England. Stayed there 2 weeks (I was so glad he went as he got there just before his mother was dying) now he is in Canada. I will be here another 2 weeks then I am being sent by plane (4 days) to New York to the big General Army Hospital there and as soon as they give me all the tests etc they will send me across country to the hospital that is just near my home.

'I am so sorry but my mother died before we were freed

as she never knew that I was alive – because that damn Lila Brooks insisted on listing me as British so the American Gov informed them that I was not alive in any internment camp. I do hope you and your family are settled and all right and that Mr Morris got work. I do hope you'll write and tell me – perhaps you have gone away. I wonder?

'… My word, when I think of how we lived, eating potato peelings from the garbage and stealing such things as vegetables etc, it all seems a nightmare in the dim past. I shall never forget all the kindness you showed me and all you did. I must say you certainly helped keep me alive – I don't know why I was worth keeping alive but it seems Providence was looking after us all the time.

'We have met many here, from North China, and they say the Japanese looked everywhere for my husband – and the terrible things they did to our servants and my animals and my gardens and home – they were so angry that they couldn't find us and the northern Japanese never knew anything about the southern Japanese – all my husband's best friends that they got they tortured to death and returned the bones in a small box to the wives…

'I do hope you haven't gone to England with all your family – Australia would be better if you did leave. Well, I must close. Please write as soon as you get this – even a note so I'll know how and where to reach you. I do hope the children are well. The Dr here told me that if you got fat (as I told him Mary was getting) he said that was not healthy and she must take lots and lots of vitamin pills every day and eat well-balanced meals and never touch tapioca at all as it poisoned your system if run down and caused a queer fat – if this reaches you within a few days write here to the hospital and if I'm gone they will forward it. If you are around any of the hotels a pilot coming to Calcutta can bring it and mail in Calcutta. I'll get it the same day – but if you have gone and this follows you, send a letter to me (Mrs A. R. Hogg) or Mrs Jean…'

It was lovely to hear from her but Mrs Hogg did more than write. In later letters, she asked Mum to send details of our clothing sizes and sent gifts of stockings and other garments which were hard to come by in post-war Britain. She was always interested in how we children were getting on and wrote very kindly of me and my sister, 'What lucky girls they are to have such lovely hair and eyes and faces – I hope they make the best of it and keep as sweet in disposition and as lovely in character as they are in appearance.'

Mum kept the letters throughout her life, touched by Mrs Hogg's recognition of her kindness when so many of the things she had done to help our fellow internees had sadly gone unnoticed.

49

HOMESICK

We did our best to make a life in England but I missed Malaya every day. I missed the sounds of Johor Bahru. I missed hearing the call to prayer that drifted out from the minarets at the start of every day and the cadences of the languages I used to know so well. I missed the smells and the taste of the food we used to eat − English food was so boring and bland in comparison. We had been brought up eating rice and in England, that was still considered completely exotic. You couldn't get it anywhere. Neither could you get a guava, or a mangosteen, or my favourite Pisang bananas. There was absolutely no chance of a piece of smelly durian fruit.

I especially missed my friends. I missed Eileen and Ozzie and the other girls in camp. I missed Pacheum and Khatijah and Keyno and Ali from the family next door in Johor Bahru. It seemed strange to me that almost everyone we saw in England was white. Though I was officially an English girl, I never felt like one. I felt very different to the children I met at the local school in Cambridge, who teased me when I couldn't find English words for something I could have expressed very well in Malay.

Within a couple of months, my father's sight had started to

get better and he too longed to be back in the Far East. He and Mum discussed going back at length. Would it be the right thing to do? Though I had missed so much schooling during my three years in the camps, I did enjoy being in class again and had won a scholarship to the technical college. I had no idea what I wanted to do but there I could study business training and learn secretarial skills such as shorthand and how to keep books. I could already type at a speed of 74 words a minute. Should they stay so that we children could be educated in the English system? George and Peter had worked so hard to catch up. We didn't know whether the schools back in Malaya were fully operational yet. Surely the convent must have closed.

In the end, it was the lack of work in Britain that tipped the balance. There was nothing for Dad to do, so just four months after we had arrived in England, Dad went back to Singapore to take up a job rebuilding the Johor Bahru hospital. It was in reasonable shape but all the balconies had to be checked to make sure that they were not in danger of falling down. Having been there when the hospital was being built, Dad knew the building better than anyone.

To begin with, we could not go with him. There wasn't enough space in the accommodation he had been offered with his new position. But not long after Dad arrived, he was given a hospital house to live in. It was just a small place but it was big enough for us all to be able to join him at last if we wanted to.

In the end, we did not go back to Malaya as a family. While we'd been in Swavesey, Mary had started a nursing course and she was determined to finish it. That meant staying in England. Mary had been encouraged to pursue a medical career by Tommy Ryan, the boy from camp who'd sent me that beautiful birthday card. Tommy was in Liverpool, studying to be a doctor. I think he also rather hoped that he and Mary would marry one day but because he was in Liverpool and she was in Cambridgeshire, they were hardly able to see one another.

Though he understood her reasons, Dad was heartbroken when Mary announced that she would not be coming back to Johor Bahru with us. But I couldn't wait to get back to the place I really thought of as home. The voyage back to Singapore couldn't come quickly enough. Every sea mile took us closer to the place I loved.

Dad met us from the ship in Singapore. It was one of the happiest moments in my life. He said, 'I'm taking you all out for lunch'.

The city was different from the one we remembered. Because there had been so much bombing, now that the debris had been cleared up, there seemed to be so many more open spaces. Still, some of the places we remembered were still there and in business, including a Chinese restaurant that used to be one of our favourites.

If I close my eyes, I can still see the restaurant as it looked that day in early 1947. On either side of the door was a flower-pot full of blooms. As you opened the door to go in, you saw the meat counter. There was meat ready and the restaurant owners had put a 'welcome' sign on it, especially for us. We went upstairs to our usual table and Dad told us we could have whatever we wanted. Our heart's desire. Me? I wanted a rice dish.

I think the moment we sat down for that meal, reunited with Dad in the place we all loved, my parents knew they had made the right decision. It was almost as if our time in camp had never happened.

50

MAKING DO

The hospital house Dad had been given was next to what had been the nurses' home. We didn't have much to furnish it with but Mum was a very strong woman who was determined to make the best of wherever we had to live. She always tried to maintain a certain level of gentility. We might not have a table – we would eat off a tea chest – but that didn't mean we couldn't have a tablecloth and proper cups and saucers.

While we were very glad to be back in Johor Bahru, reminders of the war were everywhere. Obviously, there was still a lot of structural damage to the buildings waiting to be repaired, but there were other, stranger reminders. During the occupation, the Japanese had not thought to control the local python population and the large snakes that had once been rare were dangerously ubiquitous. At the hospital there was an old zebra, presumably a former inhabitant of the city's zoo, that had been blinded by the Japanese. Everyone stopped to give that zebra something to eat as they passed by.

My brothers and I reconnected with some of the people we had come to know in camp and also with many of our childhood friends. Visiting these old friends, we would sometimes go into their houses and see furniture and porcelain that we'd had to leave behind when we were evacuated to Singapore in February 1942. Obviously, our neighbours had scavenged our things. Alam had one of our wardrobes. Josef had our mother's dresser which looked a little strange on the dirt floor of his family's hut. We didn't mention it. We tried not to begrudge our friends any of it. We knew that they had suffered under the Japanese too. The Japanese had taken their food and left them hungry. Many had fled into the forest and hid there for the duration.

I learned from my friend Khatijah that she had more or less spent the war as a prisoner in her own home. Her parents had decided to keep her hidden, lest a Japanese soldier take a liking to her and she be kidnapped and taken to work in a brothel as had happened to other less fortunate Malay girls from the village.

I remember spending time with Teddy Drysdale. During the occupation, he had been caught listening to a radio in camp and had been punished by being held in a tiny cage for days on end. Those awful times seemed very far away when we all met down on the beach at night to listen to Teddy playing his guitar. Memories of the horrors of Changi and Sime Road were slowly being overlaid with much happier memories.

There were still many Allied soldiers about Johor Bahru in 1947. I hated having to pass them on my way home from school. They were not always the gentlemen we might have wished them to be. Despite the horror of the war we had all just been through, they were far from respectful to the locals. We heard the Malays grumbling about the soldiers trying to grab hold of the Malay women as they went about their business.

Sometimes, my friend Omar would pick me up from school on his bicycle. Omar and I had known each other since we were very small and my parents weren't in the least bit worried about me associating with him. I'd climb onto the back of his bicycle and we would ride to the cold storage place where we could get a glass of milk flavoured with drinking chocolate. After that, we'd head home.

I remember once, as we were coming down the main road, a gang of soldiers spotted us and started calling us names. As far as they were concerned, a white girl shouldn't be seen with a local boy. I hated the names they called me but I was especially worried for Omar.

There was a lot of racial tension and relationships – even friendships – between white Europeans and Malayans were frowned upon. After the war, Mum would often go shopping with Pacheum, Moktar's daughter and that raised eyebrows too. People didn't seem to understand that as far as Mum was concerned, Pacheum was part of the family. But there were some shops that wouldn't even allow an Indian woman through the door.

Later, the same rude soldiers got hold of one of my brothers and made him give them the phone number of the house where we were staying. They started making prank calls at all hours, until my father picked up and told them in no uncertain terms to stop bothering us. The soldiers stationed in Singapore after the war did nothing to improve my father's view of the military.

With the hospital in Johor Bahru ready to reopen, Dad's work there was done. Next he was sent to Segamat. We moved there in the back of a two-tonne army truck, which was being used by the emergency services. We got to our new house in the middle of the afternoon. My brothers quickly jumped down from the back of the truck, but I was stuck there. Our new neighbours were waiting to greet us. One of them – the man who lived next door to our new home – came to help me down. I shooed him away. 'I can't,' I said. 'I've got a skirt on.'

I didn't need help to get off the truck but I did want to be sure that no-one saw me climbing down, in case I flashed my knickers. Our new neighbour moved everyone away so that I could have my much-needed privacy. I knew at once that he was a true gentleman.

LOVE AT FIRST SIGHT

That true gentleman was called Jim Henderson. He was our nearest neighbour. Our new house was divided from his by a hedge. Jim was a Scottish engineer in his thirties, working for the Colonial Service. During the war he had been interned in the Batu Lintang camp in Borneo. There he had suffered from such severe malnutrition that now, before he could eat, he would have to drop a small 'trolley' down his throat to open his oesophagus so that he didn't choke.

When we met him, Jim's neck was bandaged and he was having to take Vitamin B injections every day. All the same, that first evening, Jim invited us all to his house for a meal.

I soon found out that Jim loved music. That night, he put Rachmaninov on the radiogram. The romantic epic Brief Encounter, with its famous soundtrack of Rachmaninov's Piano Concerto No. 2, was one of the most popular films of the time. I went to sit by the radiogram to hear better and Jim came to sit beside me. Despite our difference in ages – he was almost two decades my senior, I found it strangely easy to talk to him.

Years later, Mum told me that, seeing me and Jim together

by the radiogram, Dad turned to her and said, 'He's going to have her.'

Mum said, 'Don't be so silly.'

But Dad had insisted, 'He is.'

As I got to know Jim better, I learned the story of his time in camp. Growing up in Scotland as a young man, he'd wanted to be a marine biologist but couldn't pass the Latin test he needed to secure a university place. He studied engineering instead. He'd gone out to Singapore in 1936 because he couldn't find work in his native Glasgow. His brother Murray had already moved to the island to work at the botanical garden.

Jim was a structural engineer. In the beginning, he took a four-year contract with the Colonial Service. At the end of those four years, he spent four months at home in Scotland, returning to Singapore just in time to get caught up in the war.

In 1941, Jim had been involved with the building of an airstrip for the RAF. He'd just finished it and passed it over when he was asked to sit on one of the newly installed guns in Singapore. Jim had never operated a gun in his life, but he was after something to do so he asked for another posting. In the end, he was sent to Borneo, to work as harbour master. He had been there for five weeks when the Japanese walked in.

Jim had returned from Scotland ready to make the Far East his home. He'd brought with him his golf kit, a piano, and beautiful crockery and linen too. One of his great friends was Jack Baker, whose family had a crockery business in Aberdeen that supplied the Royal Family at Balmoral. It was one of Jack Baker's tea sets that Jim proudly displayed in his new Borneo house.

When Jim heard that the Japanese were on their way, he quickly made plans to get away by boat with the two dalmatians he had bought as pets. He didn't make it. The soldiers arrived at the house before he could leave. They sent Jim out of the house before going inside. Over the next hour, they brought everything out onto the lawn —the precious tea-seat, the fancy linen, even the piano — and smashed it all to pieces with the golf clubs. What they couldn't smash, they set on fire.

As Jim stood there speechless, the Japanese officer in charge of the soldiers apologised to him in English.

'Forgive my men,' he said. 'They have been fighting for nine years in China. They are just animals now.'

Jim was taken prisoner. He never did find out what had happened to his dogs.

Batu Lintang, the camp where Jim was to spend the rest of the war, was housed in a former British Indian Army barracks at Kuching, Sarawak. It differed from Changi in that it contained both Allied POWs and civilian internees, all mixed in together. The population of the camp numbered around 3,000, 2,000 of whom were POWs. The men — both military and civilian — were subjected to an extremely harsh regime of forced labour. Rest days were limited to one Sunday every three weeks.

Still, Batu Lintang was the stage for some acts of extraordinary heroism. The POWs built a generator and a radio receiver, which they managed to keep secret from the Japanese for more than two and a half years. There were other smaller acts of sabotage. When the men were forced to service Japanese fighter planes, which landed at the runway they'd had to build, they added water and urine to the plane's tanks along with the fuel.

Food was always scarce. Jim told me that he and his fellow internees had been so hungry that they were reduced to eating snakes. Snails too. I knew how desperate I'd had to be to eat those. Like us at Changi and Sime Road, the Batu Lintang internees had not received most of the Red Cross parcels intended for them. Batu Lintang's Japanese medical officer, one Dr Yamamoto, even issued an order that men in the camp's hospital were to be given no rations at all. The other prisoners scraped together meals from their own meagre rations to keep the hospital patients alive. Jim found himself in that grim hospital, when he was taken ill with double pneumonia. Fortunately, a Hungarian doctor who had been interned along with him managed to smuggle in the drugs that saved Jim's life.

Jim's stories of starvation and brutality were all too familiar to me and my family, but one of his stories surprised us all because it illustrated the brutality of the Japanese towards their own. Jim said that in Batu Lintang there was a single Japanese guard who, if he could get hold of a tin or two of condensed milk, would throw it over the wire into the women's camp for the babies. When he was caught doing so by his fellow guards, he was punished by being hung by his thumbs from a tree. As if that wasn't bad enough, when he was cut down, he was put in a cage where he could only crouch and given nothing but rice and water to eat for several days.

You would have expected that level of punishment to put the Japanese guard off breaking the rules for good, but Jim told me that when the poor man was let out of his cage and was considered well enough to go back on guard duty, he went straight back to his old ways – stealing supplies to pass to the camp's most needy children whenever he could.

As was the case for us in Sime Road, the surrender of Japan did not bring immediate liberation for the internees at Bantu Lintang. That didn't come until September 11th 1945, when the Australian 9th Division together with a number of American naval officers arrived.

The Japanese guards put up no resistance and at 5pm in the camp's main square, Major General Eastick, the Australian commander, took the surrender, symbolised by Suga handing over his sword. The Japanese commandant's humiliation was complete when the POWs showed him the radio and generator – nicknamed Old Lady and Ginnie – they had kept hidden throughout their time in the camp.

Suga and the camp's highest-ranking Japanese officers were flown to Labuan to be tried as war criminals but Suga committed suicide on September 16th, robbing the POWs of their justice.

As the camp was dismantled, the surviving internees came

to learn just how narrowly they had cheated death. Among the official papers the Japanese had left behind were two 'death orders', which described how the military POWs and the civilian internees were to be executed. The first order was scheduled for August 17th. It's not known why it wasn't carried out. In the second order the executions were rescheduled for the 15th September. The women and children were to be given poisoned rice. The male civilian internees were to be shot and burned. Jim and his colleagues had escaped their fate by a matter of days. All the same, by the end of the war, two-thirds of the POWs at Batu Lintang had died through malnutrition and overwork.

52

THE CONVENT GIRL
AND THE COURTESAN

I liked Jim Henderson very much. Fortunately, so did my parents.

My father respected his opinions and vice versa. They often asked one another for advice on engineering projects. In Segamat, they worked together on repairing a bridge that had collapsed into the river and was in danger of causing a flood. On another occasion, Jim was called to fix a persistent leak in the beautiful entrance hall at the Kuala Lumpur mosque my father had helped to build. The leak had cracked the exquisite tiling. None of the engineers on the job could work out where the water was coming from but Dad was able to tell Jim exactly what the problem was. He explained that the mosque stood on the site of a spring that had been diverted so that it could be built facing Mecca. With that knowledge, Jim was quickly able to solve the problem.

On the weekends, Jim would sometimes take me and my younger brothers to the pictures. In Segamat there was a Chinese cinema that showed films in English. I loved Jim's company. It wasn't long before I knew that I wanted to spend the rest of my life with him but I was still only 15. Jim was already in his thirties.

In January 1948, I headed back to the convent I had attended before the fall of Singapore. I was going to study for my school certificate at last.

The convent was oversubscribed so to make sure that all the girls who wanted to attend were able to, it was operating on a shift system. One lot of girls would arrive first thing in the morning. The others would take over after lunch. I got a morning slot. Because the convent was quite a way from our home in Johor Bahru and getting there on time would mean ridiculously early starts, it was decided that during the week I would board in the city. Mum and Dad arranged for me to stay with April, who had become such a good friend to us in Changi and at Sime Road. April had her own property in Singapore and said she would be very happy to look after me, just as she had looked after Mary in camp. She'd be a good influence.

What Mum and Dad didn't know was that I'd recently snuck across to Singapore to meet April for a cinema outing. I rode my bicycle to the causeway. At the customs house, the officers, who knew my parents, asked if Mum and Dad knew where I was. When I admitted that they didn't, the customs officers hid my bicycle for me so I could catch a bus onwards. I met April and we saw the film. When I returned to the causeway, the customs officers had my bicycle waiting for me and I made it home without Mum or Dad being any the wiser about my big adventure.

I was pleased to be able to stay with April, who was by then in her forties. She was a very kind and welcoming woman. The only thing that puzzled me was the number of visitors who came to the house at all times of the day and night – and all of them male. I remember one night, I was sitting at the dining table at April's, doing my homework, when two RAF men called, dressed in their uniforms. One of them bid me a perfunctory 'hello' before he disappeared into a room with April. I was left in the dining room with the other man.

'Are you any good at maths?' I asked him.

My homework that night was algebra. I hated algebra. I couldn't understand why, if you had the right answer, you needed to prove how you'd got to it. I was always arguing with the nuns at school about it. I really couldn't see the point. The RAF man helped me as best he could but it wasn't long before he found himself stumped too.

'Shall we ask your friend?' I asked him, getting up to go in the direction in which April had disappeared with his mate.

'No,' he quickly stopped me. 'Best not.'

I didn't understand why he was so keen to keep me from opening that door.

A few days later, Jim came into the city for a business meeting. Having a little time before he headed back up-country with a convoy escort, he dropped in at April's house to see me. He arrived at around nine o'clock. I was already in bed. Even while living at April's I had a five o'clock start each weekday, in order to have time to shower, eat breakfast and walk to Katong to catch the school bus to be there by half past seven.

Hearing that he had missed me, Jim prepared to leave, but April stopped him. She invited him to stay the night so that he could see me in the morning. 'There's room in my bedroom,' she said. Jim was shocked. Was he hearing right? He realised at once that April was offering him more than space on a mattress. Jim knew exactly why the RAF men called night after night.

Jim was very upset to discover that April was registered as a 'comforter' – the polite phrase for sex worker. The very next day he went straight to my parents and asked them whether they knew. They'd had no idea. They found out however that April had worked as a comforter before the war. As a mixed-race woman, with no father to lend her his name, her options for employment were limited.

While my parents doubtless understood the desperation that led women like April to make the choices they did, after that it was decided that there was no way I could continue to lodge at her house. It was around this time that Jim was due to go back to Scotland on six month's leave. Now he didn't want to risk leaving me behind. He cancelled his leave, proposed marriage and set about persuading my parents that I should be allowed to become his wife the moment I turned 16.

53

WEDDING BELLS

The day after my 16th birthday, Jim and I were married.

It was a beautiful day. I wore a dress made for me by the Japanese tailor who had made clothes for Mum before the occupation. As I sat down on one of the mushroom-shaped cushions I'd loved as a child and told him what I wanted, I felt very special indeed.

For obvious reasons, the Japanese tailor was struggling in post-war Singapore. Though he had lived in Singapore for many years and was as sad about the war as anyone, there was lots of suspicion. It had been discovered that K Ba Ba, the department store we used to love to visit on a Saturday, had housed a secret Japanese spy ring.

Not only did the tailor have fewer customers, but the Chinese and Malay merchants who had previously sold him fabric were no longer happy to deal with him. Luckily he was able to find just enough white silk for my wedding trousseau. He embroidered the main body of the dress with delicate silver lilies. Fortunately, the long skirt hid my shoes. I wasn't able to find any new shoes in Singapore, so I had to wear the battered canvas ones I always wore. For a bouquet, I carried gladioli, which were the only flowers available at the time.

We didn't have many guests at our wedding ceremony but among those who did attend were some of our friends from Changi and Sime Road: Mrs Ismael, April and Muriel Shorthouse. Jim's friends Mr and Mrs Bolton came. His best man was his secretary, a Chinese man who had worked with him in Segamat. Jim's older brother Murray was also there.

We walked to the church and the ceremony was performed by the Reverend Eels, who was one of the vicars who had given the Sunday morning services in camp. Unfortunately, Reverend Eels could not stay for the wedding breakfast at my parents' house but it was a very quick party in any case. Jim and I were married at midday. By 3pm we had to be on a convoy heading up the peninsula, for it was no longer safe for Europeans to travel up-country without an armed guard.

In 1948 a guerrilla war had broken out between the communist pro-Independence fighters of the Malayan National Liberation Army and the forces of the Federation of Malaya, supported by the British Empire and Commonwealth. The Communists had a great deal of support within the local community – particularly amongst the Chinese. They were also joined by a number of Japanese soldiers who had stayed on in the region after the liberation. The devastation wreaked by the war, which had led to high unemployment and soaring food prices, made it easy to see the appeal of a communist regime.

The fierce fighting was dubbed 'The Malayan Emergency'. All European expats were basically told to stay at home as much as possible to avoid getting caught in the cross-fire.

Mum wouldn't have that. We had to go out. How else were we supposed to get to the shops or the market for food? She thought that we were streetwise enough to avoid trouble.

While I was still living at home, I would accompany Mum on her shopping trips and sometimes it was frightening. It was especially scary to be on a bus, going around a blind corner, because it had become known that was when the communists would pounce and open fire. I remember one particular bus journey when we drove straight into a guerrilla ambush. We dived down onto the floor of the bus to avoid the bullets coming through the windows and had to stay there for what felt like hours until the shooting stopped. To this day, I can't help but feel tense when I'm on a bus rounding a corner. Even in sunny Eastbourne.

But when Jim and I joined the convoy going up-country on our wedding day, I was full of excitement. Nothing could spoil our honeymoon. Or so I thought. We had not gone far into the country when we left the convoy and turned off down an unmade road. At the end of the road was an attap hut, where we were greeted by Jim's Malay cook, Haji. I followed him into the hut, to see that two camp beds had been set up for the night. It was not what I had expected.

'Is this where we're staying?' I asked.

I was desperately disappointed to see where I was going to have to sleep on my wedding night. But Jim explained that he needed to check on the nearby reservoir the next morning. He was worried that there was a blockage. Since he knew we would be passing by on our way to his house, he'd decided it made sense to stop off. He was ever practical, even on the most romantic of days. I'd soon get used to fitting in around his job.

We spent four days by the reservoir. While Jim was working, I couldn't even go for a walk without taking a pistol because there were tigers in the nearby forest. It was a strange sort of honeymoon but ultimately, I was just happy to be alone at last with the man I loved.

54

SOULMATES

I faced a lot of disapproval for going to a Japanese tailor for my wedding dress. There were also people who thought that at just 16 years old, I was much too young to be married in any case, particularly to a man of Jim's age. Jim's own brother Murray made his feelings on the matter clear. Mrs Milne, who had set up the school at Changi, also expressed her worries when she visited me after the wedding. But I doubt that the very same people who declared that I was missing out on my childhood would have worried had I been a local girl. My friend Pacheum, Moktaya's daughter, who'd been raised like a sister to me, was married at 14.

My parents actually had a larger age gap than Jim and I did. Mum was 28 when she married Dad who was 46 at the time. Plus the fact was that I'd already missed out on a childhood. Three years in the camps had seen me grow up rather quickly and I already knew that it would be impossible for me to make a life with someone who hadn't been through the same experiences. Jim felt likewise. Plenty of 'suitable' women had expressed a romantic interest in him since the war but he found he couldn't make a connection with any of them because of what he'd been through and they hadn't.

Because we had both been internees, Jim and I understood each other. That understanding made us soulmates. I knew he would not tease me for not wanting to waste even a scrap of food. He knew I would not laugh when he told me that the worst thing about being in the camp was the loss of dignity that came from having nothing to wear but a four-inch piece of cloth fashioned into a sling to cover his penis. He knew I would understand why he felt so vulnerable when naked. I knew he would understand why I felt the same way.

We didn't have to keep any aspect of our pasts hidden for fear of shocking the other. We never had to explain what we were thinking or feeling. We understood the strange triggers that brought back thoughts of camp life. But though what bonded us was our painful shared experience, we had a very happy marriage from the beginning. We had a great deal of fun together. Jim could always make me laugh. I knew as we said our vows in front of Reverend Eels that there was no-one I would rather spend my life with than Jim Henderson and that feeling never changed.

I always saw it as my role in life to care for Jim. I told him as much the day we were married. As I settled into my role as wife, I liked to make sure that he had everything he needed. Each night before we went to bed, I laid out all his clothes for the following morning. Because the damage done to his oesophagus from malnutrition meant he couldn't just eat whatever was put on the table in front of him, I would always make sure that he had soft, tasty food. I made him bread puddings and egg custard (much to the chagrin of Jim's cook, Haji, who disliked having to share his kitchen).

Jim also took a sort of food supplement drink, like Complan, to make sure he was getting all the protein, the vitamins and minerals that he needed. Sometimes, I would take Jim's lunch into work and sit with him in his office while he ate. I remember how much he enjoyed drinking coffee, which I took in for him in a bright red flask. I enjoyed my own coffee all the more simply for being in his company.

55

AND THEN THERE WERE FOUR

Shortly after Jim and I were married, we travelled back to his childhood home in Scotland for the six-month period of leave he had postponed from earlier in the year. It was very interesting for me to see the land where Jim had grown up and meet more of his relatives and friends, including Jack Baker, who claimed to have seen the Loch Ness monster. I felt very much at home in Scotland. Our first child, James, was born while we were there.

When Jim's leave was over, we returned to Malaya where he had work in Kuala Lumpur. He didn't much like the job there since it involved too much time in the office, so he was glad when he was asked to go to Jesselton in Borneo instead.

There was so much work to do in Jesselton. Every stone building in the main town had been flattened by the fighting. It was as if the war had taken Jesselton back a century or two, with little attap huts springing up where there had once been proud municipal buildings. Jim's main task there was to design and build an airport.

In the beginning, we had to live in the country club, which

sounds nice, but it was open until late so it was often hard to sleep for the noise. We moved from there into a house but it wasn't long before a typhoon tore the roof off. After that, we had to move into a little attap shack.

Jim set up a big easel in the lounge to work upon. He was in his element working on his design late into the evening. There was very little for me to do there, except care for James and sew. There was no regular contact with the outside world. It would take six weeks for post to arrive and food, likewise, was delivered every six weeks by sea. I had to cook on a paraffin stove and boil water to wash nappies on it too. I didn't even have a book to read. I was quite unhappy there. But there were little moments of happiness. We would all get up before six in the morning and sit in a cane chair on the verandah – me, Jim and James – before Jim had to leave for work. And eventually I did make friends with the doctor's wife, who had a little boy the same age as James.

Our daughter Catriona was born in Jesselton. Since there was no hospital, I had to rely on the care of a Unicef nurse who had set up a clinic in an attap hut. One morning, I went to see her before breakfast. When I arrived, she made me a piece of toast. She didn't seem in too much of a hurry to examine me, but as soon as I lay down, she told me that in fact I was moments away from giving birth. Once she had safely delivered my new baby, the nurse rang Jim and I heard her berating him, 'Fancy having to wake you up. Your daughter's just been born.'

A little later, I flew back to Singapore on a tiny prop-plane to see my family. In the clubhouse at the airport, I encountered an old friend.

'Look who's here!' said a familiar voice.

It was the mother of Buster, the baby I had so enjoyed looking after in camp. Buster stood beside her. Of course he was all grown up now. No longer a baby but a proper little boy. It was lovely to see him.

I introduced Buster and his mum to my small children and we chatted for a while. It was strange to see them out of the context of the camp and I found I felt quite shy. In Changi and at Sime Road, we'd all mucked in together, but out here – in the real world – the old social rules applied. All the same, I was glad to see that Buster was thriving – we all were – when once upon a time, it hadn't been given that we would survive our captivity.

My next flight was called. I gave Buster a quick hug and said 'goodbye'.

After Catriona was born, Jim and I decided that it was time to go back to the UK for a while. Mum travelled with me to help look after the children until Jim could follow us. He was becoming fed-up of working in Jesselton. There was so much corruption – a young civil engineer had been stealing and Jim had to report it. He was also finding it hard working alongside Korean engineers. Many of the cruellest guards at Batu Lintang had been Korean and Jim found that the daily reminder of his time in the camp was becoming too much for him.

As one of very few British civilian men in Batu Lintang,

Jim had experienced a lot of brutality. He and his fellow Brits were singled out by the Korean guards and treated especially harshly. Reminded of those awful years, Jim had to get away before he had a breakdown. He pleaded with the doctor, 'Just get me out of here.'

I think the situation might have been complicated by a feeling that Jim's experiences in camp were not fully understood or appreciated by some of Jim's colleagues at the Colonial Service, many of whom had sat out the war in safety. While we'd been in Borneo, Jim had received some money from the British Government in compensation for the time he'd been interned. He got two payments. A third was owed but didn't ever come. When Jim wrote to the Colonial Service to ask what had happened to it, he was told that the last payment would not be paid. The government was keeping the money as a 'contribution to the war effort'. The decision to withhold that money seemed to symbolise how little thought was given to the experiences of civilian internees and the ongoing implications for their physical and psychological health.

PART
SIX

Life Goes On

"It's easy to blame the Japanese for what happened, but now when I think of the people who suffered through those years I spent in the camps, I think of the Japanese soldiers too"

1949 – 2023

56

THE LONG SHADOW OF WAR

It's hard to express in writing the impact of the fear we lived with between 1942 and September 1945 and how broken we all were by the war's end. The war had changed us internees irrevocably. So many simply never recovered from the long years of deprivation and brutality.

My friend Eileen's father was reunited with the rest of the Harris family after liberation but, as Eileen put it, 'we were too ill to start living a normal life'. The whole family was sent to recuperate first in India – Eileen had typhoid – and then to England. Like me and my siblings, Eileen had never been to England before. It wasn't home to her.

The Harris family did return to Singapore quite quickly, but just four years after the end of the war, in 1949, Eileen's parents died on the same day from health complications arising from their time in the camps. Orphaned, Eileen and her siblings were sent back to England where they were fostered. Unfortunately, they were unable to stay together in the same home and were split up and sent to live miles apart from each other.

We had also stayed in touch with Gordon Shorthouse – the

young boy who had arrived in Katong without his parents
and with no memory even of his family name. Our friend
Muriel Shorthouse had kept him safe throughout our time
in the camp and afterwards he returned to England with her
and Mervyn, the son she had given birth to when we were
first in Changi. Muriel had hoped that Grant Shorthouse
– her baby's father – and she would get their 'happy ever
after' but when they got to England, Grant's family there
made it clear that they would not accept a Eurasian daugh-
ter-in-law or the 'son' – Gordon – who did not know who his
birth parents had been. Grant chose his family over Muriel
and she was left to raise Gordon and Mervyn alone in a one
bedroomed flat. More tragedy followed when Mervyn, who
had turned into something of a tearaway, climbed a pylon to
get hold of some birds' eggs, was electrocuted and was very
badly injured.

Muriel did eventually meet a man with whom she had two
daughters – Jacqueline and Elise – but she didn't want to
marry him. Not until three days before he died, when he was
lying in a hospital bed, did she finally accept his proposal.

Years later Gordon wanted to return to Singapore in the
hope that being there might help him to find out something
about the family he'd lost in 1942, but he was told that if
he did go to Singapore, he would not be allowed back into
Britain since his nationality was uncertain. In a cruel twist
of fate, Mrs Ismael, who knew for certain that she had been
born British, was not allowed to return to Britain because she
had been married to a Malayan prince, despite the fact that
her husband had been killed by the Japanese. These were the

arbitrary ways in which people continued to be separated from their loved ones for years after the war.

There were other awful stories of life post liberation. We heard of one English woman who, knowing that the occupation was coming, had left her baby girl with her ayah – a Malay woman – hoping that in this way she could keep the baby safe from harm. At the end of the war, the English woman returned to her old home to reclaim her daughter but the Malay family who had looked after the child for three years refused to let her go. They went so far as to claim that the English child had been theirs all along. They had dyed her hair dark and browned her skin. The girl had no idea that she was not Malay. The Malay family were all she had ever known. The war had turned her birth mother into a stranger.

Meanwhile many male internees in particular sometimes felt ashamed of their time in camp while others suffered from health problems that simply would not go away. We heard of one man who, for 28 years after he was liberated from camp, kept getting a strange rash on different parts of his body at the same time every year. When he finally went to the School of Tropical Medicine to have the rash investigated, he discovered that it was caused by a tropical worm that had lived inside his body for almost three decades. It caused a rash when it came to the surface of his skin to mate. The diagnosis was confirmed when a nurse treating the rash saw movement beneath his skin. It was the worm trying to find a mate again.

Another internee had come back from the Far East with

tropical boils that he just couldn't seem to get rid of. When his daughter was born, she too was covered in boils that she seemed to have inherited from her father. Fortunately, in her late teens, she went to the School of Tropical Medicine who were able to cure the boils at last.

These were the continued humiliations former internees had to live with.

There were some attempts at restitution. In March 1946, a war crimes trial was held in the Supreme Court Building in which 21 former members of the Kempeitai were tried for their part in the atrocities that followed the 'Double Tenth', when 57 internees were tortured – 15 of those to death. At the end of the trial, which lasted three weeks, seven of the Kempeitai were acquitted, six were given prison sentences varying from eight years to life imprisonment. The remaining eight, including Lieutenant Colonel Sumida, were sentenced to death. The news was welcomed by many former Changi internees.

'Double Tenth' prisoner Dr Cecily Williams went on to do great things after the war. As a young doctor, she had written a thesis on childhood diseases in Africa's Gold Coast. Among the conditions she observed was one of advanced malnutrition caused by lack of protein, which had the name 'kwashikor' in the local Ga language. Dr Williams' research was interrupted by her time in the camps, but afterwards she took it up again. In 1948, she became the head of the World Health Organisation's Mother and Child Health department, where she concentrated her efforts on tailoring healthcare for the poor to local resources. She also lectured on Mother and Child Health in over 70 countries worldwide.

Dr Williams' fellow 'Double Tenth' prisoner Freddy Bloom and her husband Philip moved to London after liberation. Philip became a consultant obstetrician and later a psychiatrist. Meanwhile Freddy set up the 'Youth Book Club', a not-for-profit group designed to introduce teenagers to good books. Mary used to see Freddy from time to time and she helped my sister to apply to nursing school.

A little later, Freddy had a daughter: Virginia. As a result of the malnutrition Freddy had experienced during the war, Virginia was born deaf. However, Freddy was determined not to let that hold her daughter back, spending many hours teaching Virginia how to speak. She documented her experiences – and Virginia's success – and brought them to the wider deaf community via the National Deaf Children's Society. Freddy devoted herself to the Society and in 1966 was awarded an OBE for her services to deaf children. In 1980, she published an account of her time in Changi, entitled Dear Philip: a Diary of Captivity, Changi 1942-5.

Despite everything she experienced at the hands of the Kempeitai, Freddy Bloom never allowed herself to hold any hatred towards the Japanese people. For Freddy, as the old saying goes, 'Living well was the best revenge.'

I hoped to do the same.

57

MORE TRAVELS WITH MY FAMILY

Back in the 1950s, after a short period in the UK, Jim and I moved with our children to Dar Es Salaam in Tanzania. I loved it there. I threw myself into the Tanzanian way of living, taking James and Catriona on the bus into town with the local women and children, who regarded us with kind curiosity. I wish I'd been able to learn more of the language, so that I might have made some friends. As it was, I learned only a few words. James and Catriona picked up more, calling the insects and animals they encountered by their Swahili names.

After Tanzania, we returned to England, where Jim went to work for the Ministry Of Defence, looking after three American bases, including Alconbury, which he loved.

Cyprus came next. I enjoyed living on the island, but while we were there, Jim became very ill (more complications from his treatment in camp) and we decided to go back to my family in Cambridgeshire to have our third baby, our daughter Joanna. We bought a house near to my mother and brothers. Dad was still in Singapore at this time but Mum had had enough and moved back without him. With the guerrilla war still raging in Malaya, she thought that it would be safer for my brothers to grow up in England.

We were living in Huntingdon when our fourth child, another daughter whom we called Jessie, was born. I would have happily had two more children but we were moving all the time. Jim couldn't seem to settle. He was too used to being abroad. He did love Scotland and had often said he'd like to retire there but it was complicated being so close to the wider Morris family.

As I've mentioned before, our shared experience in the camps meant that Jim and I had a level of understanding between us that was not possible with people who hadn't been through the same thing. This was starkly illustrated by Jim's post-war relationships with the people he had known in Scotland before he left for the Far East. He could no longer relate to the friends to whom he had once been so close. It was even worse with his brother.

It was because of his brother Murray that Jim had gone out to Singapore in the first place. Murray was working for the government, in one of the municipal gardens. However, as soon as war broke out in the Far East, Murray was evacuated on the grounds that he had knowledge and information that might be valuable to the Japanese. Upon evacuation, he took his family to South Africa, where he worked in the botanical gardens. In doing so, he had escaped being taken prisoner and avoided the worst of the war.

The huge difference between Murray and Jim's wartime experiences created a big rift between them, where they had once been so close. In the years after Jim and I got married, each visit to my in-laws would repeat the same sorry pattern. It would begin with a short period of friendly patter about family and friends in common before descending into what felt like hours of uncomfortable silence as the brothers separately contemplated the twist of fate which meant that Murray had spent the war among his flowers in South Africa while Jim and I had starved under the Japanese occupation.

Jim didn't ever talk about what had happened to him in the camp with the people back home, but the knowledge of it hung in the air between them and us. After the first 15 minutes, there was literally nothing left to say. How could there be? We would travel home again wishing that things might change for the better but knowing they never could.

In Aberdeen, Jim saw a future unfolding in which he might be asked to take on family responsibilities that he didn't want. So one day, when we were sitting in the lounge together at the end of the evening, he suddenly announced, 'We're going to Australia.' All I could do was nod in agreement and start getting ready for another move.

In Australia, Jim took on a role in water conservation, which he loved as it meant he could be outdoors all day every day. He was forced to retire from the position at 60 but we still had Jessie to put through school. In order to pay for that, we moved back to London, where Jim took a job in Whitehall. It was an office job and he didn't much enjoy it.

Because Jim and my parents had been worried about my living with April, I'd left school without finishing my school certificate. Since then, I'd been a very busy wife and a mother, but as the years went on I felt that I needed something more. After Jessie was born, Jim was very ill and spent four months in Papworth Hospital. While he was there, I got to know some of the nursing staff very well and started to wonder whether nursing might be the right job for me too.

I saw an advertisement in a local paper, inviting people to apply for nursing training. My education was patchy. In all, I'd only had about nine uninterrupted months of formal schooling, but I had learned quite a bit from helping my children to do their homework. I wondered if the knowledge I did have would be enough. To my delight it was and I was accepted onto the course. I trained in general nursing, district nursing and later to be a theatre nurse.

Because I had to do the course part-time to fit around the family, it took longer than it might have done and I had to give up nursing training while we were in Australia, but though I did not know it when Jim turned 60 and we moved back to England, it would not be long before I needed my new qualifications.

58

A HAPPY EVER AFTER
CUT SHORT

The war had not only fractured Jim's relationship with his brother, it had also broken his relationship with God. The things he had seen made it impossible for him to believe in a benign creator. How could the bottomless cruelty the Japanese had meted out to us in the camps ever be part of some divine plan?

I think, in truth, that half of my husband had died in Batu Lintang. As a young man in Scotland, Jim had played the organ in church. Now he refused to go inside the 'house of God'. Neither would he play the piano. He simply could not do it anymore. Yet, when we were living in Swavesey, seeing that the churchyard there was in a terrible mess and overgrown, he bought gardening equipment so that he could tidy it up.

I did manage to persuade Jim that he must go inside the church when our daughter Catriona was married, aged 21, but that was the only time (Catriona was attached to the church. From the age of 10, she'd taken part in the services and joined the Red Cross). When Jim took our other daughter Jessie to Sunday school, he would drop her off and pick her up, but he would never cross the threshold.

Even golf was something Jim could no longer enjoy, since picking up a set of clubs only reminded him of the Japanese soldiers ransacking his house in a frenzy at the beginning of the war. When our grandson James was nine, he asked Jim to teach him how to play but Jim would not go near a golf course. When our granddaughter was learning to play the piano and got stuck on her scales, I said, 'It's a shame your grandfather isn't here. He could have helped you.' I realised as I said it that our daughters didn't even know that their father could play.

The war had robbed Jim of so much. I think that ultimately it robbed me of a long and happy marriage too. When Jim retired from Whitehall, we decided that we would go to live in Scotland at long last. It had been his long-cherished dream to spend his retirement there. We bought some land, found a builder and got planning permission to create our dream home. In April, we travelled up there to meet the builder. We were ready to start work.

Jim had driven us up to Scotland. Though I knew how to drive, when we were together, Jim always liked to be behind the steering wheel. On the way back, however, he asked me if I would mind taking over. It was a small thing but I sensed that it was not a good sign. Shortly after that Jim's health started going downhill again and he went into hospital.

I remember sitting by Jim's bed on the ward and him holding my hand, looking into my eyes and telling me with a smile, 'I fancy you just as much as I did when we first met.'

It might sound glib, but though Jim was never given to flowery speeches, I knew how much he loved me.

Ours was a true and lasting love. Despite what some people may have thought about our age gap, we had been very happy over the years we'd had together. Mr and Mrs Bolton, friends of Jim's who said upon our marriage, 'She's a very lucky girl', had been right.

Jim died not long after he was admitted. I had asked the staff at the hospital to make sure that they did not give him any food – I told them that I would bring it in – but one day they went ahead and gave him scrambled egg and mashed potato and that was it. He was only in his mid-sixties when he died. By no means old. But those three years of malnutrition in Batu Lintang had taken their toll and finally caught up with him.

Two uniformed representatives of the Air Ministry attended Jim's funeral. I was surprised to see them but I was also glad. I think Jim would have been pleased to know that his contribution over the years had been noticed and appreciated.

Jim's death was devastating for the whole family but especially so for our children. James, Catriona and Joanna were pretty much grown-up but Jessie was still at school when her father died.

I had thought that Jim and I had years of happiness ahead of us, but suddenly I was a widow with a young child to provide for. I couldn't put Jessie through the upheaval of a move to Scotland on top of everything else. I knew I had no choice but to halt the building work (thank goodness the builder had got no further than digging the footings), put the land in Scotland up for sale, stay in the old house and find myself a job.

I was relieved to discover that I was able to go back to nursing.

When Jessie finished school and went off to Edinburgh to train as a nursery nurse, my own rebooted nursing career gave me a focus that helped carry me through the worst of my grief. I very much enjoyed working in theatre. I would go in before the surgeon arrived and make sure that everything was set up ahead of the day's scheduled operations. I'd make sure that all the theatre wellies were clean, set up the equipment and the trolleys, making sure that the surgeon had three sets of tools ready. I mostly assisted on ear and nose operations. Helping people gave me the strength to carry on.

59

WHAT CAME NEXT

Twenty-five years after the war, the whole Morris family was back in the UK. Dad had died in Singapore shortly before he was due to retire, but the rest of us were 'back home' as Mum called it.

I wasn't the only nurse in the family. My sister Mary, who had stayed behind in England to train as a nurse when the rest of us returned to Johor Bahru in March 1947, had excelled in her career. Nursing suited her firm but caring manner. She became very senior and was well-respected by her colleagues. The young doctor who dared to tell a nurse to 'chop chop' within Mary's earshot won't have forgotten the telling off he got in a hurry. Mary had married Vic and had two children – a son and a daughter.

When my brothers came back to England with Mum, they were both over 14 so were not able to enrol in school. 14 was the leaving age for most English students at that time. They had to find work.

George, the youngest of us Morris siblings, joined the milk marketing board, where he met a young woman called Violet. The offices of the milk marketing board were on a very busy road, so at the end of each day, George would walk

Violet across to safety. They soon fell in love and married – I made the wedding dress and outfits for four bridesmaids – and set themselves up as farmers, living in a caravan on their land. Although he had to leave school early, George still loved learning.

Every night, after work, George would get out his books and try to continue his education that had been cut short when he came back from the Far East. Eventually he trained to become a teacher and taught metalwork at a technical college. He once won a prize for building a rickshaw from three metals, welding them together in a way which other people said could not be done.

George did not live to a great old age, The organ damage he had sustained from growing up malnourished in camp caused him health problems throughout his life. Finally, his heart gave way. He was survived by his three sons, Anthony, Jonathan and Nicholas, who take great interest in the family history.

My brother Peter was known for his jovial personality in camp and he retained that happy outlook all through his life, despite his difficulties. He was a keen cook. After the war, he found himself in a restaurant where some Malay men were trying and failing to cook roti. 'Let me show you how to do it,' Peter said. Before he knew it, there was a queue. Peter loved food. He especially loved my mince pies. He once ate 36 in one sitting. Around the Christmas season, he would always have at least six pies warming on top of the boiler.

When he came back to England, Peter was eligible for

national service so he joined the RAF. It was the start of a long career. At the age of 21, he got married to Rosemary, who was working as a nanny in the village where we lived. Due to the injuries he sustained in camp, Peter was unable to have children but he helped Rosemary to raise her daughter from another relationship. Eventually, Peter and Rosemary divorced but she remained a good friend. Peter remarried to his second wife Doreen.

Peter was always very smartly dressed and fastidious. He found dirt distressing and when we visited his house, I always made sure the children were on their best behaviour and didn't make a mess. Looking back, I can see how that must have come from our time in camp, when it was so hard to stay clean. Peter never forgot about the maggots that had infested the sores on his legs.

Like George, Peter died much too young, from skin cancer, undoubtedly caused by being forced to work out in the Singapore sun all day long when he was just a 10-year-old child, living in a prison camp.

60

KEEPING THE MEMORIES ALIVE

Some people who were interned in the Far East during World War II don't want to remember. A short while back, I had an unexpected encounter in an embroidery shop with another woman who had been a child prisoner in Changi. Of course I went to talk to her, but seeing me only seemed to cause her distress. The young relative who was looking after her that day dragged her away from me, warning me, 'Don't upset her. Thinking about that time makes her upset.'

I recognised the way she felt and understood how time had not blunted her emotions. My brother Peter hated the Japanese people and anything to do with them for the rest of his life. He could never forgive them for what had been done to him. When as adults, my siblings and I talked about our time in the camps, it was clear that Peter was the most upset. I don't think any of us would have disagreed that he had the worst experience, separated from all of us in the men's camp when he was just 10 years old.

In many ways, I shared his anger. Not only at the Japanese but at the way we had been treated after the war by the

British establishment. The way we were so often over-looked.

There's a sense that, even now, the Second World War in the Far East is the 'forgotten war'. While everyone is familiar with the story of the war in Europe and knows about the Nazi atrocities in the concentration camps such as Auschwitz, Bergen-Belsen and Buchenwald, the plight of the men, women and children taken captive by the Japanese is much less well-known.

This is changing. In recent years, more efforts have been made to recognise the ongoing hardships of the Far East Prisoners of War (FEPOW). Organisations such as the British Legion have successfully campaigned for compensation. Personally, I have found that the annual gatherings of the various FEPOW associations have been very helpful to me in processing our painful shared experience.

I have been back to Singapore many times over the years; I've joined memorial services and laid two wreaths there to honour the people who were lost. On one occasion, I laid a wreath with my friend Wilma, the girl whose family had been made to wear red circles in a Japanese version of the Nazi's Star of David symbols for the Jews. The last time I was in Singapore, eight years ago, a Japanese minister, Mr Toyah, came to the memorial ceremony and gave a speech of reconciliation.

It's easy to blame the Japanese for what happened, but now when I think of the people who suffered through those years I spent in the camps, I think of the Japanese soldiers too. They were mostly very young men. Many of them had never been out of their village before they were sent to fight. They were cannon fodder. Just like the Allied soldiers, some of them were only teenagers when they were sent to their deaths so far away from home.

These days there is a museum at Changi dedicated to the people who were interned there. The chapel built by the male internees has been preserved. In 2002, the site of the Sime Road Camp was designated a historic site by Singapore's National Heritage Board. Though Hut 16 and the other buildings that were our home in 1944 and 1945 have long since been torn down, a sign explains the importance of the location.

It's not only in Singapore that museums have been working to raise awareness of what happened. While visiting Australia some time ago, I heard that someone had made a donation related to FEPOWs to a museum in Perth. It turned out to be the first skirt the girls guides made in Changi. It was sewn as a costume for a concert. It was a fan skirt and we had each signed our names on it. You need a magnifying glass to be able to read them, but all our names are there: Mine, Eileen's, Shirley's, Evelyn's. Everyone in our group.

Closer to home, the quilt that I helped to make for Mrs Ennis, our girl guide leader, is now in the Imperial War Museum in London. I went up to London to see the presentation. The Australian ambassador was in attendance. I was glad to see the quilt again but it was frustrating to see that the names of so many of the people who had been at Changi and Sime Road were missing from the wider display. It's important to me that the world knows who they were.

I wished that Mum might have been there to see that exhibition at the IWM. I still wish that Mum's contribution to the welfare of everyone in the camps had been recognised with something like a CBE. To my mind, she served her country just as well as any soldier. But there were no medals for most of the women and children who spent the war in Changi and Sime Road. I was struck by the importance of such symbols when I was invited to the opening of a monument dedicated to the Far East POWs at the National Arboretum in Alrewas in Staffordshire. With one of my friends, I waited in line to be introduced to Prince Charles, as he was then. As the Prince got closer, he suddenly swerved away from us to greet a group of veterans who were all wearing their war medals. Without outward signs that we too were veterans of a sort, we weren't even on his radar.

I am happy, though, that the Far East POWs have their own monument at the arboretum – a Malay-style house, containing an exhibition about our internment – at long last.

61

THE POWER OF FORGIVENESS

Mrs Mulvany, who brightened all our lives in captivity, showed in her later life that compassion is the best cure for hatred, which ultimately only eats away at the person who feels it. I have always tried to follow her example. It hasn't always been easy. But I remember clearly the moment when I thought I might be reaching a place of true forgiveness at last.

A few years ago, while I was on my way back from a service at Westminster Abbey to commemorate the end of the War in the Far East, I had an experience that seemed perhaps to be a sign or a message that it was time to let go of some of my pain.

At the end of the service, I decided that I would take the tube back to Kings Cross, from where I would catch a train home. I had a vague idea that I needed to take the Northern Line, so I headed to the underground station where I found myself staring at the enormous tube map in total bewilderment. As I stood there, I was conscious of someone standing beside me. When I turned, I saw that it was a middle-aged

Japanese man. We locked eyes and without thinking, I bowed at him, bending at the waist as automatically as I had done as a child. He bowed back, clearly amused and delighted to find that this white woman of a certain age knew how things were done in Japan.

'Can I help you?' he asked me. 'Where do you want to go?'

I told him my destination.

'Ah,' he said. 'In that case, you need this line.'

He pointed it out on the map.

'And I will walk you to your platform,' he insisted.

He was so polite yet so clear that he wanted to help me, that I let myself be led. We stood on the platform for a couple of moments before the train I needed drew in. The Japanese man watched to make sure that I boarded safely. The driver warned us all to 'stand clear of the closing doors'. In the middle of the carriage, I stood and looked back at my Good Samaritan and as the doors of the tube train swished back together, we bowed to one another once again.

That man knew none of the reasons why I might have wanted to hate him. He had seen me as a fellow traveller, a fellow human, and only wanted to help. I thought about him for a long time as I made my way back home.

Recently, I've been thinking about that encounter on the tube platform a lot. Writing this book has certainly made me revisit some memories that I thought I'd filed away for good. Though most of my recollections of those three and a half years I spent in Changi Jail and Sime Road are painful, I can look back on the years before and immediately after the Japanese occupation with affection, as I remember my early childhood in Tampoi and Johor Bahru, then, much later, meeting my husband and falling in love. Singapore is different now. It's a much more commercial place than it was when I was a child. Everything is about money. But if I could close my eyes and wake up anywhere in the world, it would still be in Johor Bahru.

These days I live alone in Eastbourne. Knitting and crochet – the skills my mother taught me and my friends before the war – are still hobbies of mine. I am part of a small group of women who get together every week to knit and chat over coffee. I knit clothes for the discarded plastic dolls I find in charity shops. Once the dolls are dressed, I pass them on to my granddaughter Emma, who takes them into the school where she works as principal. Some of the children she teaches come from such disadvantaged backgrounds that they arrive at school not knowing how to dress themselves or even, in some cases, how to name their own body parts. Using the dolls, Emma can help them to learn the words for eyes, noses and mouths, or how to do up buttons and put on socks.

In a cabinet in my living room, I still have the photographs that my mother saved when we were evacuated from Johor Bahru in January 1942 and my paper doll, who looks as pretty and pristine as she did on the day that I made her. She is tucked inside an old exercise book from the convent school, along with the dresses I designed for her. But I also have a memento of the war in the Far East that perhaps you wouldn't expect to find in my home.

In 1975, I met one Mr Robertson from Montrose, a voluntary driver at the hospital where I was working, who had served with the RAF in Burma, India and Japan during the war. Mr Robertson told me about a 'souvenir' that he had picked as he walked through the devastation of Hiroshima. He told me how he had been shuffling through the debris, kicking at it as he went, when he kicked a piece of molten glass that rolled over to reveal something special hidden underneath. He showed me the glass. Perhaps once upon a time the melted mass had been a green bottle. He turned it over and there, just as he had found it, was a small porcelain cat, nestled like a kernel in a nutshell.

Mr Robertson invited me to pick the little cat out of its green glass bed. On her bottom, she had a thin layer of ash, but released from the glass, she was otherwise perfect, coated in pure white glaze with painted grey patches on her paws and ears. Her eyes were closed and her mouth was upturned in a quiet and peaceful smile. Her tail was curled around her and she looked perfectly at peace.

'You can have it,' he said. 'I know how much you like cats.' He'd heard that my own real cat, Sugar, had recently died.

I have it all these years later. That little cat in her bed of molten glass has come with me from house to house. When I pick her up, I experience a multitude of feelings. I feel such sadness for the people of Hiroshima and Nagasaki, the men, women and children who died there, and yet I know that had the Americans not dropped their atomic bombs on those cities, my family and I would not have survived the war.

There is so much conflicting emotion in my heart, even

now: anger, sadness, relief and perhaps even survivor's guilt. The cat brings back memories of all the people who did not make it through the war and reminds me that I did. That I lived to tell my story and my whole family came out of the camps alive. I've travelled the world and had a career I enjoyed. I married the man I adored. I have four children of whom I am very proud and many grandchildren and great-grandchildren who fill my life with happiness. I have known love. I have survived.

EPILOGUE

In April 2023, I was able to see the quilt we made for Mrs Ennis at Changi once again. These days the quilt is kept behind the scenes at the Imperial War Museum in London, but my friend Simon Robinson arranged for me to make a private visit with my daughter Catriona, my granddaughter Emma and my great-granddaughter Bella, known as Bea. Bea had recently turned 13 – just a little older than I was when we were liberated from Sime Road.

The Changi quilt is under glass now to keep it from fading. It was hard for me to see it properly with the lights overhead reflecting in the protective cover, but with the help of the torch on Simon's phone, I was gradually able to pick out the names of my long-ago girl guide friends. As I read each name, the memories of the girls who had embroidered them came back to me as clearly as if we'd left the camp only yesterday. There was Ozzie. And there was Eileen. There was Nellie, who died when she was knocked off her scooter five years after we were liberated.

'How does it make you feel?' my granddaughter asked me. 'Seeing the quilt again?'

In truth, it made me feel very sad, to see those names,

knowing that of the 20-odd girls who sat in a circle to sew that quilt there are very few of us left now. But I was glad to be at the museum with three generations of women from my family, supporting me as I said a last goodbye to those embroidered squares so full of memories.

As we studied the faded fabric flowers, the making of which had kept us going through those dark days in Changi jail, my granddaughter Emma told me about the quilt she has been making using replica 1940s fabric in the same 'grandmother's garden' pattern that the Changi girl guides followed. Then she told me that she felt that my husband – her grandfather – was with us at the museum that day too. I think she was right. Jim was there with us in spirit. And perhaps Mum and Dad and my brothers George and Peter too. That idea made me feel very happy indeed.

Acknowledgements

I'd like to thank all the people who have helped me to put this book together over the past year. Thank you to Simon Robinson, for finding me a publisher, to Chris Manby for helping to shape my story, to my editors Paul Dove and Christine Costello at Mirror Books, to my nephew Anthony Morris for helping with the photographs, and to my children, grandchildren and great-grandchildren for their love and support.

Pieces of the Past

*Cuttings and documents from a time
gone but never forgotten...*

WRITE VERY CLEARLY ON THE LINES TO AVOID DELAY IN CENSORSHIP

DATE *June 8th 1943*

*My dear Nora at long last we have
found your whereabouts, we are
greatly relieved. I happy, to
know you + Harry are safe.
altho in Japanese hands.
We heard from your Mother
through the Red Cross. She, + all
of us, had been so worried
about you all Nora, not having
any news. It was good news
indeed. We do hope the chil[dren]
are also safe + somewher[e]
near you. We are anxiou[s]
now for further news. Th[...]
that you may soon be [...]
to write home. All you[...]
are well. I hope you are too*

BOTTOM PANEL

TWO "ASIA BOYS"

TO those of our readers who
were interned at Changi Gaol
and Sime Road internment
camps, "the Asia Boys" has a
familiar ring, says the October
number of "British Malaya."
Most will remember one of
them, Tommy Ryan, who was a
cabin boy on the *Empress of
Asia.* This boy studied hard in
camp and was coached by members of the Malayan Education
Department.

He matriculated in camp and
has since been given a scholarship at Liverpool University where
he is taking a medical course.

Many will also remember the
young Eurasian boy, Donald
Newman, who, on the strength of
his internment results, gained [a]
scholarship at Coventry Technic[-]
al College, and recently passe[d]
out 2nd in his School Certifi[-]
cate examination.

LOST LETTERS A very rare letter (*left*) – the only one the
Morris family received in camp through the Red Cross,
months after it was posted and (*right*) a newspaper
cutting about Tommy Ryan

THE CONVENT-SCHOOL, JOHORE BAHRU

SCHOOL DAYS At the age of six years and three months, I started school, following my big sister to the Johor Bahru outpost of the Convent Of The Holy Infant Jesus

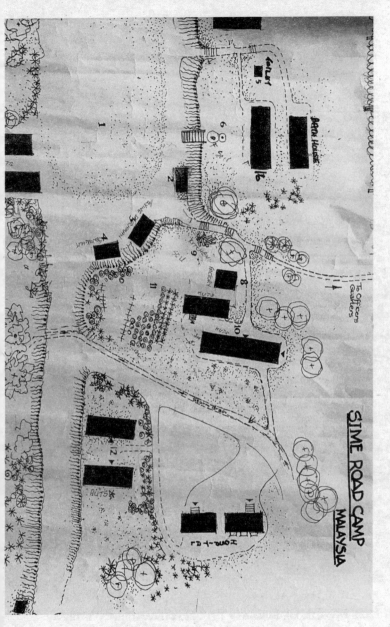

DIAGRAM Sime Road Camp, drawn by Alison Ewan

1. Name. Olga Morris.
2. Born at Singapore.
3. On March 28th 1932.
4. She is a subject of British
5. Height. 4ft 5"
6. Colour of eyes-. Brown.
7. " " hair. " "
8. Special marks.-none
9. Date of internment- Feb. 20th 1942.
10. Remarks.-none

1. Name Peter Morris
2. Born at Singapore.
3. On June 10th 1934.
4. British
5 Height 4ft 3".
6. Eyes Blue
7 Hair Fair
8. Special marks none.
9. Interned Feb. 20th 1942
10. Remarks-none

1. George Morris
2. Singapore
3. Nov. 27th 1935
4. British
5. Height 4ft 1"
6. Eyes, Blue
7. Hair, fair
8. Marks,-none
9. Feb. 20th 1942
10. Remarks-none

M.E.H.

LAST MINUTE DOCUMENTS We didn't have a birth certificate so our mother had to write our information down on a piece of paper ahead of our repatriation voyage

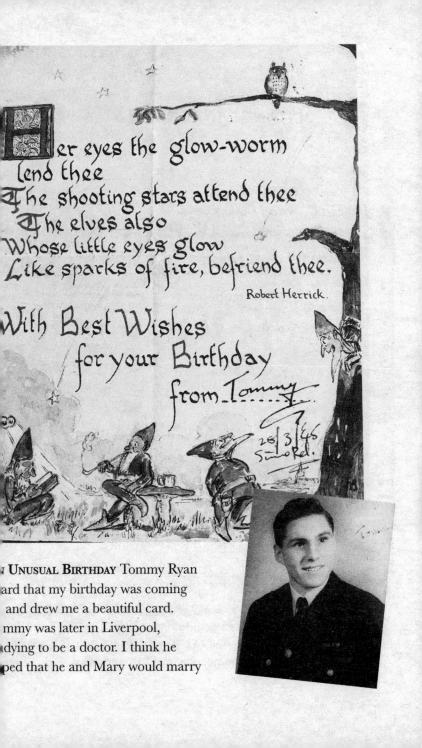

Her eyes the glow-worm lend thee
The shooting stars attend thee
The elves also
Whose little eyes glow
Like sparks of fire, befriend thee.

Robert Herrick.

With Best Wishes
for your Birthday
from Tommy

28/3/46
S...o Rd.

AN UNUSUAL BIRTHDAY Tommy Ryan
...ard that my birthday was coming
... and drew me a beautiful card.
...mmy was later in Liverpool,
...dying to be a doctor. I think he
...ped that he and Mary would marry

CHANGI INTERNMENT CAMP,
SYONAN

♣♣

Document
of
Identity

♣♣

Women's Camp

No. 2557

Mary Morris
Kuala Lumpur
June 28th 1929
. British
. Height 5 ft 3"
. Eyes - blue
. Hair - fair
. Marks - none
. Feb 20th 1942
9. Remarks - none

DOCUMENTATION My mother's and sister Mary's identity papers from Changi with her name, date of birth and physical descripti

THIS IS TO CERTIFY that the person whose signature appears opposite states that his/her name is **MORRIS Nora**

that he/she was born at Over Cambridge on **Sept. 26th 1897**

that he/she is a **British** subject

and that we after enquiry have reason to believe that these statements are correct.

Signature of Camp Commandant: *M. E. Hopkins.*
B.Sc.(Lond.), M.R.C.S., L.R.C.P.

Date 6.11.42.

PARTICULARS:

Height 5 ft. 4 ins.
Colour of eyes Blue
Colour of hair Fair
Special marks —
Occupation Housewife
Period of residence in Malaya 22 years
Date of internment Feb 20th 1942
Reference
Remarks Husband a Lawyer

N Morris.
Signature of Holder

Right thumb-print of holder

TO ALL ALLIED PRISONERS OF WAR

THE JAPANESE FORCES HAVE SURRENDERED UNCONDITIONALLY AND THE WAR IS OVER

WE will get supplies to you as soon as is humanly possible and will make arrangements to get you out but, owing to the distances involved, it may be some time before we can achieve this.

YOU will help us and yourselves if you act as follows :—

(1) Stay in your camp until you get further orders from us.

(2) Start preparing nominal rolls of personnel, giving fullest particulars.

(3) List your most urgent necessities.

(4) If you have been starved or underfed for long periods DO NOT eat large quantities of solid food, fruit or vegetables at first. It is dangerous for you to do so. Small quantities at frequent intervals are much safer and will strengthen you far more quickly. For those who are really ill or very weak, fluids such as broth and soup, making use of the water in which rice and other foods have been boiled, are much the best. Gifts of food from the local population should be cooked. We want to get you back home quickly, safe and sound, and we do not want to risk your chances from diarrhoea, dysentry and cholera at this last stage.

(5) Local authorities and/or Allied officers will take charge of your affairs in a very short time. Be guided by their advice.

LIBERATION The good news eventually arrived in the form of hundreds of leaflets, dropped from allied planes. As the leaflets began to flutter down over Sime Road, we rushed to grab them